Praise

'I thought Barnsley w... Michael Parkinson un... collection of soulful vi... ...o and live there!' Rich ..., playwright

'This book is Barnsley through and through: tender, funny, and beautifully real. A true celebration of the voices that make us who we are.' **Kate Rusby, folk singer and songwriter**

'The pieces in this collection resound with genuine authenticity of place and character, this is the heartbeat of South Yorkshire. Writing so full of the stuff of life you can almost taste it.' **John Godber, playwright**

'LUNG's work continues to challenge and inspire the nation, consistently creating bold, deeply human work like *Calling Barnsley* – a timely collection of monologues that bring real voices vividly to life.' **Indhu Rubasingham, Artistic Director, National Theatre**

'Barnsley – my home town. Best Town Hall, best Market, best everything in fact. Barnsley made me a tough, ambitious, cultured, proud Yorkshirewoman. She served me very well and this book proves I'm not alone in loving our little town.' **Jenni Murray, journalist and broadcaster**

'A whole spectrum of memories and experiences with our little town and its people at the heart. Poignant, emotional, human.' **Milly Johnson, author**

'*Calling Barnsley* does what LUNG, and strong communities, do best. These monologues weave specific, individual human lives into a collective experience that still lets every voice shine. It's a brilliant achievement by LUNG, and by Barnsley – and whether you know the place or not, it's for you.' **Chris Thorpe, playwright and performer**

'This collection of stories from the citizens of Barnsley, which happens to be my hometown, are as varied, vivid and resonant as they are important to read. The marginalisation of what the political class calls "ordinary people" in the literary and media space can sometimes mean that nefarious actors with loud voices are able to misrepresent this cohort in unflattering ways. As well as much else, *Calling Barnsley* serves as a corrective to this troubling trend. As it is elsewhere, all human life is here.' **Ian Winwood, author and journalist**

'By amplifying the voices of people whose stories should more often be told but rarely get heard, Helen Monks and Matt Woodhead have placed themselves at the vanguard of a thrilling new generation of young English theatre-makers. Always challenging, never boring, increasingly relevant, LUNG always demands nothing less than our full attention.' **Darren Henley, CEO of Arts Council England**

'How brilliant is this! A book filled with the voices of Barnsley people about experiences that have meant so much to them. It's a bit like catching snippets of familiar conversations, immediately putting me back in my comfort zone with words that really resonate. For this book expresses the feelings of a place far too often ignored by the mainstream, but presented here in all their power as the authentic voice of our wonderful town.' **Professor Joann Fletcher, writer and Egyptologist**

LUNG presents

CALLING BARNSLEY

by Helen Monks and Matt Woodhead

Calling Barnsley was first performed as an audio installation in a public phone box at Barnsley Civic on 16 January 2025.

CALLING BARNSLEY
by Helen Monks and Matt Woodhead

Audio Cast
Madiha Ansari
Paul Atkins
Kay Elúvian
Dermot Daly
Jem Dobbs
Danielle Phillips

Creative Team
Owen Crouch — Sound Designer
Helen Monks — Writer
Lulu Tam — Designer
Rachael Walton — Engagement Officer
Matt Woodhead — Writer & Director

Production Team
Joe D'Souza — Engineer
Ethan Hudson — Production Manager
Jack Helliwell — Recording Engineer
Camille Koosyial — Producer

Creative Associates
David Andrew
Jeremy Birtles
Dominic Brown
Rebecca Hipwell-Stafford
Josh Hoyle
Thomas Hughes
Amelia Jones
Evie McGowan
Sky McSeveney
Lizzie Race
Ruby Scattergood
Joe Wheeliker
Luca Wildgoose

Academic Advisor
Dr Ryan Bramley, University of Sheffield

Acknowledgements

Storytellers

A heartfelt thank you to everyone who shared their story and made this book possible. Barnsley is teeming with tales of resilience, strength and joy. It's such a privilege to share these messages far and wide.

Supporters

With gratitude to all of the supporters of this project: Paul Atkins, Katie Battcock, Devon Blood, Clare Bushby, Joel Brogan, Jon Finch, Ruth Hannant, Liane Holdsworth, Beck Howell, Tom Lucas, Gemma Nixon, Mark Starling, Coby Walsh, Jason White and Dan Winder. A big thank you to Lily Levinson and the team at Faber & Faber for your belief in these stories and the people of Barnsley.

Community partners

Our appreciation to everyone who took part in our *Calling Barnsley* workshops. Action for Autism Barnsley, Art Works, B:Friend, Barnsley Creative Writers, Barnsley Youth Council, Barnsley Recovery Connections, Beacon South Yorkshire Carer Support, Birkwood Primary School, Creative Recovery, Game Changer, Hoyland Springwood Primary School, Hoyland Nether Rangers, Inclusive Action, Oasis Coffee Morning, Outwood Academy Shafton, Outwood Primary Academy Littleworth Grange, Royston St John Baptist CE Primary School and Together at the Table.

Residency affiliates

A special thanks to everyone at Feels like Home and The Salvation Army in Goldthorpe for hosting our residency workshop programme.

Our funders

Calling Barnsley was originally commissioned and funded by Storying Barnsley in partnership with Barnsley College and Barnsley Civic. Legacy funding was provided by Barnsley Council's Great Childhood Ambition and Love Where You Live programmes.

Our sponsors

We are grateful to our *Calling Barnsley* sponsors, Longley Farm.

Additional credits

LUNG is a National Portfolio Organisation, supported by Arts Council England.

LUNG

Founded in Barnsley in 2014, LUNG is a campaign-led arts charity, working UK wide to make hidden voices heard. We are a National Theatre Resident Company and partners with The Lowry in Salford.

Our work takes multiple forms:

- We develop high quality verbatim productions that tour from theatres to school halls to the Houses of Parliament
- We create educational and training resources for teachers, social workers and people in power
- We spearhead award winning campaigns to spark change

Our plays are published by Faber and Faber and studied on the AQA GCSE Drama Syllabus. We believe in the value of art to amplify untold stories and its power to transform the world around us.

Core team

Rachael Brimley	Development Manager
Jo Brown	Assistant Producer
Milla Jackson	Development Manager (Maternity Cover)
Sarah Kadri	Producer (Communities & Campaigns)
Nur Khairiyah Binte Ramli	General Manager
Lauren Yvonne Townsend	Producer (Productions & Artist Development)
Helen Monks	Co-Director
Matt Woodhead	Co-Director

Associates

Madiha Ansari	LUNG Creative
Gitika Buttoo	Associate Director

Board

Shazad Amin	Trustee
Rachel Clarke Ederle	Trustee
Inga Hirst	Trustee
Euginia Lolomari	Trustee
Zeena Rasheed	Chair
Deborah Rees	Trustee
Gilly Roche	Trustee
Rhiannon McKay-Smith	Trustee

To find out more, visit www.lungtheatre.co.uk, or follow us at @lungtheatre

Barnsley Civic

Barnsley Civic is a dynamic, modern arts centre based in a historic location in the heart of Barnsley. Our building has been synonymous with the arts and culture for nearly 150 years. The complementary threads of creative learning, community support and public entertainment have always been part of Barnsley Civic and its history.

Today, our building houses a theatre, studio theatre, art and design gallery, and multiple events and community spaces. Our diverse programme encompasses the widest range of performing and visual arts. And, as the key local civic and cultural space, we also support a wide range of community, voluntary and cultural organisations from across Barnsley and South Yorkshire.

To find out more, visit www.barnsleycivic.co.uk or follow us @barnsleycivic

---

Barnsley College

Barnsley College is a recognised centre of excellence in further and higher education, with a proud reputation for nurturing creativity and talent. The College equips students with the skills, knowledge and confidence to succeed in their chosen careers.

With a commitment to inclusivity, Barnsley College provides opportunities for students from all backgrounds to excel in a wide range of pathways and sectors. Its dedicated staff and strong community ethos ensure that every student is supported to reach their potential and make a positive impact on the world beyond education.

To find out more, visit www.barnsley.ac.uk or follow us @barnsleycollege

Storying Barnsley

Storying Barnsley was a community focused cultural initiative funded by Arts Council England's Cultural Development Fund and delivered by Barnsley Council. Running from 2022 to 2025, it fostered cultural participation, supported local creatives, and strengthened the creative sector. The programme included creative commissions, workshops, exhibitions, and public art projects, engaging over 37,500 people and directly involving 4,890 participants in creative activities.

Storying Barnsley helped local artists develop their skills, set up cultural networks, and contributed to Barnsley's cultural strategy. By focusing on community collaboration and creative experimentation, Storying Barnsley has brought people closer together, empowered local artists, and laid the groundwork for a sustainable and inclusive cultural future in Barnsley.

Storying Barnsley was delivered by Liane Holdsworth and Coby Walsh in partnership with the incredibly talented, dedicated and creative artists and communities of Barnsley.

To find out more, visit www.barnsley-museums.com/projects

Calling Barnsley

Helen Monks is a writer and actor. She co-wrote *E15*, which has been on two UK tours and was published by Bloomsbury. Her play *Trojan Horse* was developed with Leeds Playhouse and her musical *The Children's Inquiry* won the Sky Arts Award for theatre. Selected acting credits include: *Upstart Crow*, *Inside No. 9* (BBC 2), *Election Spy* (BBC 1), *Genius* (21st Century Fox) and *Raised by Wolves* (Channel 4).

Matt Woodhead is a writer and director. He trained on the National Theatre Studio's Directors Course and as a trainee director at Leeds Playhouse. Writing credits include: *The 56*, *E15*, *Who Cares*, *Chilcot*, *Trojan Horse*, *Woodhill* and *The Children's Inquiry*. Selected awards include the Director's Guild Award for Best Newcomer and the John Fernald Award.

by the same authors from Faber
THE CHILDREN'S INQUIRY

also by Matt Woodhead from Faber
WOODHILL

HELEN MONKS AND MATT WOODHEAD

Calling Barnsley

faber

First published in 2025
by Faber & Faber Limited
The Bindery, 51 Hatton Garden
London, EC1N 8HN

Typeset by Brighton Gray
Printed and bound in the UK by CPI Group (Ltd), Croydon CR0 4YY

All rights reserved
© Helen Monks and Matt Woodhead, 2025

Helen Monks and Matt Woodhead are hereby identified as authors
of this work in accordance with Section 77 of the
Copyright, Designs and Patents Act 1988

All rights whatsoever in this work, amateur or professional,
are strictly reserved. Applications for permission for any use
whatsoever including performance rights must be made in
advance, prior to any such proposed use, to
Curtis Brown Group Ltd, Cunard House,
15 Regent Street, London SW1Y 4LR

No performance may be given unless a licence
has first been obtained

This book is sold subject to the condition that it shall not,
by way of trade or otherwise, be lent, resold, hired out
or otherwise circulated without the publisher's prior consent
in any form of binding or cover other than that in which
it is published and without a similar condition including
this condition being imposed on the subsequent purchaser

A CIP record for this book
is available from the British Library

ISBN 978–0–571–39756–3

Printed and bound in the UK on FSC® certified paper in line with our continuing
commitment to ethical business practices, sustainability and the environment.
For further information see faber.co.uk/environmental-policy

Our authorised representative in the EU for product safety is
Easy Access System Europe, Mustamäe tee 50, 10621 Tallinn, Estonia
gpsr.requests@easproject.com

2 4 6 8 10 9 7 5 3 1

Contents

A Few Words on Barnsley by Ken Loach 7

Foreword by Ian McMillan 9

Authors' Note 11

Calling Barnsley 13

Afterword by Dr Ryan Bramley 139

Get Support 141

Resources 142

A Few Words on Barnsley

I first saw Barnsley through the eyes of the writer Barry Hines. Three words caught its spirit: strength, struggle and laughter.

The strength comes from the work of those who dug for coal; the struggle was against their exploitation by their employers, whether the coal owners or the Tory governments; and the laughter is from their sharp observation of the contradictions of daily life and work.

Barry relished all three aspects of the town's spirit. He captured them in his love of the Barnsley language, its words and rhythms. It is the language of resistance and comedy, and it is always a joy to hear.

Ken Loach, 2025

Foreword

MOOR RATTLE THAN A CAN O' MABS

I was on the 219 the other day going from Darfield into Barnsley; the bus was pretty full and I got sat behind two women who, as far as I could make out, hadn't seen each other for ages and were catching up. It was like being in the audience at a storytelling festival as memories piled on anecdotes piled on tales and then poured themselves liberally over impersonations of long-lost school mates. Sometimes, gloriously and with a kind of language-abundance, they both spoke at the same time, laughing as they did so. It was a joyful journey.

Eventually we rolled into Barnsley Bus Station and one of the women looked out of the window; 'Bloody hell, I was supposed to get off at Kendray!' she said, and I knew then that this would be the start of another story the next time the two met: The Time We Went Past Kendray.

And that is what is at the heart of this wonderful book: stories. Here are Barnsley people telling their lives in sentences and paragraphs that shine and sing. Here is abundance and nuance and deep feeling and gags that encapsulate truths. There's a myth, a strong and persistent myth, that Barnsley people (particularly Barnsley men) don't talk much about anything; that we are strong, silent types – like pitstack versions of Mount Rushmore faces.

This book proves the opposite: that we are people who love to talk and that we tell our lives because our lives are worth telling. And we tell our lives because we want to be listened to, and we want to listen back to other people's lives.

Each morning I go for my early stroll which ends at 6 a.m. at the paper shop. I meet two other early blokes and we carry the papers into the shop. Then we stand for a while and 'kall', which is a grand old Barnsley word for the art of gossiping and nattering. We have, as they say round here, 'moor rattle than a can o' mabs'.

One of us is slightly deaf, and so we have to enunciate and make ourselves clear and it struck me one rainy morning that we were like a chorus in a Greek drama or like a group of people in a Shakespeare play, making theatre from the everyday, holding folks up for praise or ridicule, and turning the everyday into something epic and meaningful. 'See you tomorrow,' we say to each other and we go our separate ways. Until the next day.

Enjoy this book. Enjoy it so much that you miss your stop on the bus. And then, of course, tell your own stories, because I know you've got plenty.

See you at the paper shop.

Ian McMillan, 2025

Authors' Note

THIS ONE'S FOR YOU

To write this book, we've met people from every corner of this town. We've run workshops, hosted coffee mornings, arranged play dates, gone on walks, met in pubs, churches and school halls – we've even followed farmers through their fields. Wherever we went, whoever we spoke to, we always asked the same question:

'Do you see yourself as creative?'

Almost every time, the answer was the same – a resounding yes.

Because Barnsley isn't just full of stories. It's full of storytellers.

The voices in this book come from real conversations with the most joyful people – creative, generous, funny, fierce and full of life. These monologues are built from interviews, but what's been captured goes beyond words. It's the spirit of a town that knows exactly what it is.

One of the final people we had the privilege to speak with was Dickie Bird. It was just days before he passed, but his energy never wavered. He spoke with love and humour, sharing memories of the two great passions in his life: cricket – and Barnsley.

There's a statue of Dickie in town, with his finger raised – a proud symbol of Barnsley's spirit. But we're certain Dickie would agree: every single person in this town deserves a statue.

Not all heroes are cast in bronze. This book may not stand in the town centre, but it stands for the town. It's a way of preserving the stories and celebrating the gorgeous souls we met – and the many more we didn't.

Barnsley – this one's for you.

Helen Monks & Matt Woodhead,
Co-Directors of LUNG, 2025

CALLING BARNSLEY

Stories haunt this mining town,
waiting to be heard.
Whose voices are we missing,
in this place that we call home?

Calling Barnsley was first performed as an audio installation in a public phone box at Barnsley Civic on 16 January 2025. The cast was as follows:

Madiha Ansari
Paul Atkins
Dermot Daly
Jem Dobbs
Kay Elúvian
Danielle Phillips

Sound Designer Owen Crouch
Recording Engineer Jack Helliwell
Production Manager Ethan Hudson
Producer Camille Koosyial
Engineer Joe D'Souza
Designer Lulu Tam
Engagement Officer Rachael Walton
Director Matt Woodhead

Guidance

This book can be read as a series of bite-size stories, or performed as monologues.

Numbers

In our phone box installation, audiences are invited to step in, dial a number and hear a story. Each story has been given its own unique number, to capture the dates, times and other digits that stand out in people's lives.

Performance

This book is packed with brilliant voices, waiting to be brought to life. If you are performing these stories, ask yourself:

1. Who are you speaking to?
2. What are the turning points in the story?
3. How are you different at the end of the speech to the person you were at the beginning?

Bring your own interpretation to the character you are playing, and most importantly of all, have fun when you're doing it!

Accents

Barnsley is a melting pot of accents and dialects. We've heard from voices that hail as far as Sierra Leone to down the road in Stairfoot. If you haven't been to Barnsley before, there are plenty of stories to get your teeth stuck into. And if you know Yorkshire, you'll spot that 'wor' means 'was' or 'were'.

Content

Some stories contain content that some readers might find challenging, including the subjects of addiction, coercive control, death and grief, domestic violence, racism and self-harm.

O: INFINITE

I moved in with my grandma, in Darton. My room was smaller but the view out the window. Wow. I could see Barnsley Town Hall, right in the distance and at night I watched as all the colours changed.

It started at school. I remember sitting in lessons and I just couldn't engage. I just couldn't focus. I wanted to be somewhere else. To avoid the pain my mind would drift. Wander. It started as daydreaming. Then over time, it became almost obsessive. I got to the point where I was living completely in my imagination. I'd created an alternative reality. In my head.

My dad was driving me along in the car, but he wasn't my dad. He was my security guard. And there were cars like, driving alongside us, but they weren't just any cars. These cars were escorting me, to keep me safe, on my way to the very important event I'd been invited to. I was famous. And I was the richest person. My life was amazing, my life was so amazing, in my head.

I needed to get back. I had to come back.

There's this spot. This one spot. On the way to Sheffield. It looks out over. Well, everything. You're so high. So high up. You can't hear sounds but you can see it. See everything. And because of the bend in the hill it's like looking through a tilt-shift lens. Have you seen those? They make everything miniature. You're big and the world is small and you can sit up there, almost like a god, and look down and see and understand. Process. What am I escaping from? Face it. Bring me back.

Imagination is so important. But I'm glad that I live back in reality.

1: IT BEAMED

It's on top of a hill. And it's white. And I have so many memories of seeing it, like, there, up there on top of the hill, lit up. The sun hits it. And it beams.

My dad always had a motto about Barnsley Hospital: 'It's the place where all of our relatives go in, but very few come out.'

My grandad had this cough. I always just thought it was like a nervous tic or like a character thing or something. Yeah, he had an oxygen tank and he carried it around with him. I didn't think owt of it. He'd always been fine, right?

It happened so fast. Grandad, he suddenly went downhill. And before I knew it – he was sent to Barnsley Hospital.

My mum had gone ahead and she called the house phone. She said, 'You need to get here – now.'

Me and my dad hared it into town. There it was, on top of the hill, bright white, beaming.

We walked in the main entrance and I said to my dad, 'Is it left or is it right?' I wish I'd trusted my instinct. I wish I'd trusted my gut. My dad was like, 'I'm sure it's right.' I knew it was left.

We turned right. Down the straight, straight, straight corridor. Into this massive lift. Up, up, up until we came out and realised, we were in the neonatal ward.

Quick. Hurry. Back down in the massive lift, back down the straight, straight corridor, back to the main entrance, and this time, we turn left.

Moment we stepped out, a nurse comes out of my grandad's room. And she's like, 'I'm so sorry. You've missed him. He just died.'

I watched as all the blood just slowly drained from his face. I watched his flesh turn from pink to blue. It was like, I can't explain it. It was like uncooking a ham.

If only I'd trusted my instinct. If only I'd trusted my gut. If only I'd turned left rather than right, I would have seen him before he died.

Dad drove us home, out of town. I looked back behind us and there it was, on top of the hill. Standing, like it always did, like nowt was different, like nowt had changed. Bright white. Lit up. And as the sun hit it. It beamed.

2: SCARS

Scars are something to be proud of, they show the journey of your life.

My memory is quite foggy, but from what my mum told me, I almost died when I was two. We'd just moved to Barnsley and mum was letting me just run around ASDA because I was a free spirited child. My favourite outfit was my cute little Juicy Couture tracksuit, bright pink. I had a hat on, sunglasses over my eyes and I was running down the clothing aisle.

At first I didn't cry, I was like, 'Whoa, what's just happened?' When I realised I'd run headfirst into a metal clothes rack and proper impaled my head, that's when I started to cry.

Mum was swearing and insulting people, she does that when she panics. The ambulance wasn't coming, I mean they never do round here, and I was bleeding. There was so much blood.

When the ambulance finally arrived, this paramedic was trying everything to stop me crying. He got this rubber surgical glove and blew it up. I looked at him and Mum was like, 'She's stopped' – but then I started crying all over again.

The paramedic glued the crack in my head, put me back together again and sent us on our way. I didn't need stitches, but I do have this round dome scar in the middle of my forehead. It feels like the moon. Not crater and rockery but a tiny circle you can just brush with your finger.

A lot of people want to look young forever. They freak out when they get marks on their skin, but not me. I've got scars on my knees from when I fell off my scooter, I've got a scar for my nose piercing because it never healed and I've got scars on my arms too. I used to self-harm because, just because.

Scars are something to be proud of, they show the journey of your life. My scars tell the world that I made it and I'm still alive. And that girl in the Juicy Couture tracksuit – she has many more journeys left to go.

3: KEBAB

It was cold, probably around three in the morning. I was with a few old college mates. I can't remember what the occasion was, but we were dressed smart. Not tuxedos and bow ties smart. Dirt cheap blazer off the sale rack at Burton's smart.

I'm walking towards the taxi rank when I felt something hit me on the side of my head. I look down and there's a kebab just lying on the floor. Must have only had two bites out of it. I knew the sauce was garlic mayo because I was wearing half of it. I turned towards one of the nearby shops and there was this random guy. And as kindly and politely as I could, I was like, 'Why did you throw that kebab at me?'

The guy's partner wades in. I think they were having an argument before I arrived and this whole thing seemed to bring them together. Anyway, it's all effing and blinding and she's like, 'Leave him alone, leave him alone!' And I'm like, 'What about me? I'm the victim here!' And my mates are all like, 'Just walk away, just walk away.'

In these parts if you are wearing anything a little bit fruity, you are sticking your head above the parapet: 'Don't wear a rucksack to school or you'll get bullied.' 'Don't wear a My Chemical Romance jumper or you're a mosher.' 'Don't wear cherry red shoes to match day or people will take the mick.' 'Get out of Barnsley – you don't belong here with your fancy blazer!'

I wish I had the courage to wear what I wanted to wear. If you take it off, you let them win. But then again, if you keep it on, you're in for a harder life. So, it's easier to just take it off.

I walked away. Got in a taxi. And to this day, I don't think I've worn a blazer or anything like that in Barnsley again.

4: TIME WAITS FOR NO MAN

Dad used to have this saying – 'Time waits for no man.' In life, you don't know how long you've got left.

Growing up, we always had my dad to rely on, until a few years ago. Then, very slowly, we got these little signs. He'd invite us round for Sunday dinner, but when we got there it wasn't cooked. He'd never missed a birthday, but he stopped giving us cards and presents.

Caring for someone feels like being stuck down a well. You're trying to climb up to reach the light, but you just keep falling. Dad was diagnosed with Alzheimer's and vascular dementia. It's so hard seeing someone who's looked after you all your life slowly fade away.

I don't know what Dad is going to be like from one day to the next. I have to be prepared to listen to the same story over and over again or he might get confused and wander off. Dad went through a phase where he got really nasty, so I had to learn to step out of the room and hold my breath.

There are moments when the fog lifts. Dad's now wheelchair bound but we get him in a taxi and down the pub. When we get the karaoke going, you can't knock him down. He's got four songs he loves to sing: 'Dirty Old Town', 'Annie's Song', 'The Fields of Athenry', and 'Danny Boy'. I can't count how many times I've heard them, but every time my heart still skips a beat. Even when he hasn't got his glasses on and he can't see the screen, Dad remembers all the words.

I'm preparing myself for the day that I walk into a room to a blank face, and he doesn't remember who I am. But I know the dad he used to be. The dad who'd take us for picnics at Langsett Res. Dad who we'd toast marshmallows with in the woods. Dad who'd come in from the garden smelling of conifers and freshly cut grass.

Time waits for no man but I'm going to cherish the time what we have left.

5: THE CHRISTMAS LIGHTS OF THURNSCOE

At one time, the local working men's club here was the richest working men's club in England. When the pit closed, the village became a bit of a ghost town. Back then there was no work, no infrastructure. How do you cope? What do you live for?

We're on the frontier here, on the border between Rotherham and Doncaster so people have sometimes felt a bit lost. After the strike, the story of Thurnscoe was very much one of people moving away.

All roads in Thurnscoe lead to the library, which is where you'll find me. We've a local residents' group which meets here, in the heart of the village. The group is a great mix of people. We've got professional people, retired people, we've even got the local vicar. Our mission is simple – to make Thurnscoe a better place to live.

At first it was hanging baskets, community clean-ups, quite small stuff. But after a while, we started thinking about our legacy. Before the lockdown, we had twelve, fifteen people come to our meeting and the decision was unanimous. There'd never been a Christmas lights switch-on in the village before. The council couldn't afford it. So we got to work.

Of course, we had those little anxieties, 'Will it get vandalised?' 'Will the lights get smashed?' 'What if someone nicks the baubles off the tree?' But we had to do it, we had to change the story.

In the car park of the library, we stood under the Christmas tree. At first no one came, but one by one, people started to gather.

Five!

Another face.

Four!

Another face.

Three!

Another face.

Two!

Another face.

One!

Another face.

The countdown ended, the Christmas lights came on and the crowd let out an enormous cheer. Outside the library were hundreds of faces, young and adult, all lit up. And in those beaming faces I saw hope.

The story of Thurnscoe was very much one of people moving away but our lights sent a message. We've had some hard times in the past, but our future is bright. Now, the story of Thurnscoe is one of people coming together, of people coming back.

6: THE PIPE

One, two, three, heave.

My mum said I was the rogue of the family. What you might call nowadays – ADHD.

It was a Sunday morning and me and a mate decided to go play in the backfield of our council estate. There was a blocked up bridge but it had a gap you could climb through. We called that the monkey tunnel. There was an old railway tunnel we'd go in to tell stories. We called that the ghost tunnel. And then there was the pipe. It was used for water drainage or something.

One, two, three, heave.

We had toy cars that we were trying to make loop-the-loop on the inside of the pipe. My mate, Ronnie, his car went too fast and went racing inside. Racing down the pipe.

One, two, three, heave.

I was six, so small enough to go in and get it. As I was crawling backwards, my foot got caught. It got stuck. I got stuck.

One, two, three, heave.

First thing I thought was, I'm going to get in so much trouble. Ronnie tried to wiggle me out for about half an hour but it just wasn't working.

One, two, three, heave.

Ronnie went and got my Uncle Mark, who turned up with his shovel. I knew it wasn't going to work. He tried to smash the pipe from above, digging it and mashing it. It was no use.

It was pure concrete. Uncle Mark realised – he'd have to grab my hands and heave me out.

One, two, three, heave. One, two, three, heave. One, two, three, heave. And – out I came! Thank God. I was free.

When I came out, the fire brigade and police turned up. I don't know who called them but all I thought was, 'Oh no, what's my mum gonna think?'

And then, this guy from the *Barnsley Chronicle* arrived. He asked me to get back in the pipe for a picture. He said, 'It's fine, kid, you'll be right.' I'd just got out the pipe and I didn't even think twice about it – there I was, getting right back in again.

My mum always said I was the rogue of the family. And now we had the picture to prove it.

8: BIKE LIGHTS

It's November, it's dark and it's early evening. I'm just about to head out the door to hang about with my mate when Mum is like, 'You're not going out on your bike without your lights.' We'd had cycling proficiency training at primary school and I was like, 'You know what, fair enough.' Mum replaced the proper chunky batteries and off I go.

It's around eight o'clock in the evening and I'm pedalling up this hill in the middle of Elsecar. It's not massive but the bike is heavy, so my breath is going. I hit the T-junction. I look left and I see this coach coming down the road towards me.

It's dark, so I put both feet on the floor, hands on the handlebars, I keep to my side of the white line and wait to see which way this coach is turning. I wait for it to pass, I wait for it to pass, I wait for it to pass and then I see the coach is turning the corner and swinging towards me. I hear the revs of the engine getting louder and louder and I'm like, 'This sounds really close.' Then I hear this massive crunch.

I wake up on my back, looking up at the stars. I hear screaming, then realise it's me. The coach had stopped, and people are coming out from their houses. My bike looks like a boomerang, just completely concaved.

I'd a fractured wrist, my left ankle was shattered, I was in a proper bad way. This woman kneels down and asks, 'Who can I call?' There's a red telephone box on the edge of the hill so I stutter out the number of my mum.

When you're growing up, you're told all sorts, aren't you? 'Eat your greens.' 'Don't leave the crust on your bread.' 'You better be good, or Father Christmas won't come.' But it doesn't work like that does it? Life isn't always fair.

I mean, you can do your cycle proficiency training, you can change the batteries on your bike lights, you can wait on the right side of the road but it doesn't always matter does it? You're still getting hit by a bus.

9: FIND SOMETHING YOU LOVE

Find something you love.

My brother played football for a local under elevens. I loved football. The manager, Mr Sterling, I used to annoy him, annoy him, annoy him until eventually he threw a shirt at me and said, 'Come down on Sunday.' By eight year old I wor starting every game. By time I wor nine I wor captain.

Find something you love.

One day, we got a knock on door. 'Is Jamey in?' My mum wor like, 'Oh no what's he done now?' They said, 'No he hasn't done owt, we've seen Jamey play – and we want to sign him.' My mum turned around, 'How much are subs?' 'A pound a week.' 'I'm not paying that.' So that wor it. The thing I loved. I couldn't do it.

Find something you love.

I always had a feeling something had been wrong. It was only the other week my brother put it into words. He said, 'You never had a chance in life. You grew up knowing you wor never really wanted.' I can see now, he's right. I had three older brothers and I just knew, I wasn't supposed to have come along.

I'd get bullied all day at school and then come home and be bullied there too. There wasn't space for me. I wasn't wanted. So no wonder I was stopped from doing what I loved.

Find something you love.

As I got older I had this friend. We were inseparable. We used to go round to his cousins on a Friday night when his mum and dad were at the pub. He had decks. Yeah, he had decks.

That's when I started DJing. I loved it. And this time, no one was gonna stop me.

Find something you love.

My youngen, would you believe it, he's just been accepted on a scholarship at Barnsley Football Club. It costs two hundred pounds a year but I've always made sure, if he loves it, that's what he does.

Find something you love.

For me, it couldn't be football. But I found music. It's kept me alive. I'm still DJing now. I can just go, switch my decks on for an hour, two hours, and forget about everything.

If something gets in your way, or someone tries to stop you, well then you might have to make a turn. But just find something that you love. Find something you love. And don't stop doing it.

10: WHO REALLY IS YOUR NEIGHBOUR?

As a kid, Barnsley was a no-go area. I tried going to play football. My friends were like, 'Ethan, you're with us, you've got nothing to worry about.' The moment we arrived it was all, 'Who brought him down here?' I was the only Black guy on the football pitch. Within ten minutes, we were on the bus back to Sheffield.

I came back to Barnsley as a youth worker. The first group of young men came up and touched my fist. I had to sort of challenge the stigma in my head: 'It's going to be dangerous; it's going to be racist.' To be honest, in Barnsley it could go either way.

I once ran a session that culminated in kids chanting a white power song to us. Eight of them and they all knew it word for word. 'We are the white warriors.' This wasn't something they'd just seen on Facebook or whatever. They'd clearly sung this before.

There's some young people who've called me names that don't even belong in my generation, never mind theirs. I've had to ask my grandad what some of these words mean.

You only need to look at the news. Nigel Farage was in town, going round with a bus. He knew, Barnsley's a community he can target. Poverty breeds contempt. People are looking for someone to blame.

A few years ago, there was an EDL march in town. There was a guy, like the ringleader, drumming everyone up and I recognised him. I called Mum and said, 'Do you remember my friend Mikey, the one with the ginger hair?' Mum goes, 'Oh that lovely young lad who used to come round for dinner?' I said, 'Yeah Mum, he's leading an EDL march.'

The people on these marches though, they're people in our community who only really show their cards when Tommy Robinson arrives or when there's riots like the ones in the summer. It's not just sons of miners who hold these views – it's a lot of middle-class people too.

You think you know them, but who really is your neighbour?

12: THE BRIDGE TO NOWHERE

Have you seen the new bridge in town? My neighbour says it cost twelve million pounds. It's gross, it's gold and it goes to nowhere.

I was on my lunch break, so I thought I'd pop to Greggs and get myself a sausage roll. I walked past the bridge to nowhere and something caught my eye. A crowd beginning to gather.

I shuffle my way to the front and there was this man, standing in front of a plaque. I turn to the woman next to me and ask, 'Who's this fella then?' She tells me it's Prince Edward and my blood starts to boil. He makes a speech about the people of Barnsley and declares the bridge open. I try not to scream during the applause.

I'm standing right at the front of the line and as the Prince goes to leave, he catches my eye and the cameras are on me. 'This is it,' I tell myself. 'This is it.' I take a deep breath and go to speak, but the words won't come out.

I want to ask him how he sleeps at night? Having so much, while so many have nothing. I want to ask what it feels like to add an extra hole to your belt, while asking us lot to tighten ours. I want to ask him why his bloodline is better than mine? But my tongue gets tied. I just say nothing.

Prince whatever leaves and the crowd follows. I turn to the bridge, then I look back at the Prince. The bridge. The Prince. The bridge. The Prince. Both gross, both gold, both tricking us into going nowhere.

13: I TOLD YOU SO

I came here to spite my mother. She was like, 'Just stay near. Go to Rotherham College.' But I was not a happy chappy. I didn't really know myself. Confused, a bit everywhere, so I was like, 'No, Mum, I need my independence. I've gotta get out, I'm gonna do it. I'm gonna go Barnsley.'

First day of college I spent the whole bus journey like, 'I don't know if I like this.' The fear, the situation, the realisation of something new.

I buy a Fanta and get Google Maps going. And I'm looking around like, 'This is so weird,' because in Rotherham it's just grey building, grey building, burnt-down building, grey building. But this place actually looks better. All the buildings are like big and red.

College is on a hill and it looks huge. I'm afraid to go in and I'm like, 'This is crazy, what am I doing?' I'm like so early, I've got ages, and I don't want to talk to anyone so I go and sit in this little park. There's a memorial and benches so I just sit and wait.

Go on my phone. Yep, no messages. Sit and listen to The Cortinas to remind me of home. Go on my phone again. Yep, still no messages. Maybe Mum is right? Go on my phone. Yep, still no messages. Should I stay or should I go back to Rotherham?

Thirteen minutes before I need to head over.

Twelve.

Eleven.

Ten.

Nine.

Eight.

Seven.

Six.

Five.

Four.

Three.

Two.

One.

Time to go. I stand up and I walk straight through the doors.
The second I go in – it's like some sort of weight is lifted.
I hate to say it, Mum, but I told you so.

14: FULL CIRCLE

As a boy, at weekends, I'd get up, go out the back door, go out in nature and not come back. I've always loved nature, me.

Dad was a miner and at fourteen I'd go down to the pit like, to see the pit ponies. I also rode on conveyor belt where the coals come out. Horses wor supposed to be white, like. But down there, they'd turned black. Yes it wor a mine but, because of the ponies, it still felt like nature to me.

The mine's closed. Ten or so years later, my dad died – coal, he had coal dust on the lungs.

I was a steelworker until I was replaced by a robot. I worked in the youth centres but they closed them down. I worked as a mental health visitor and then the contract got pulled. I thought, what, what, what am I going to do now? I was scared to death.

When I stopped work I was having problems with my health.

I went back. Back to the pit. At first, you couldn't see owt. Shafts capped and it was covered in nettles. But I cut it all back. And I planted so many trees and shrubs and different things.

Then rabbits and deer come and eat them all. But it's okay. I start again, plant more, plant more. Trees, shrubs, things. Until the place is covered in nature.

Eventually, I got a scan. A scan over the chest. They said, 'You've got coal. Coal dust on your lungs.'

Full circle, you could say that. I've come full circle. It's taken time but it's a lovely site now. So much nature over where the mines used to be. And I've always loved nature, me.

16: PENISTONE PRAWNS

My dad used to buy these frozen prawns on the market, all packed into a big cube. You couldn't see a single prawn. Just a block of pink.

I wasn't keen on school, I much preferred being out of it. Smoking behind the toilets, sneaking off, spending my dinner money at the chippy. I got hauled into the head's office, they'd got plans for me but I didn't have any of those plans. I was going to leave school at sixteen because it was boring.

I couldn't go out drinking as a teenager in Penistone because everybody knew me. So I used to get absolutely hammered in the pubs in Barnsley town. In those days we used to drink Babycham and Cherry B. On the bus home I was violently sick. Red Cherry B everywhere. Everyone thought there'd been a major incident.

Penistone is like another world. It's just people walking around with their eyes closed. I mean it's fine, it's lovely, but it's such a small, packed environment. I woke up one day and I thought, 'This isn't very good, is it?'

I went to night school, got workbooks in the post, watched television programmes at ridiculous hours in the morning. It opened my eyes. I couldn't be content in a small world. I couldn't be content being somewhere that's famous for its train station and for being the coldest place on earth. I couldn't do it anymore. So I woke up one day and walked away with a suitcase.

My dad used to buy these frozen prawns on the market, all packed into a big cube. You couldn't see a single prawn. There's more to life than Penistone and its big block of pink.

18: STILL SINKING

When I first got together with Daniel, he took me to Blackpool. I was in the water, and I started to drown. I shouted, 'Get me out, I'm sinking!' and Daniel just laughed. The Coastguard had to come out to rescue me.

Daniel was a food pleaser. I tend to stuff my face, like a comfort thing and he'd overfeed me. Takeaways every night, chocolate fudge cake, millions milkshakes, jam roly-poly. I didn't realise, but I was still sinking.

Ariana came into the world with loads of dark hair and baby blue eyes. I'd always dress her in bows and frills. One look at her just melted my heart. I didn't realise, but I was still sinking.

Daniel controlled who I knocked about with. When he went out working, his dad would come round to watch me. If someone came to the door, I had to leave it. I didn't realise, but I was still sinking.

I was pregnant with my second child when Daniel put the cameras up. I couldn't leave so I'd just sit on the sofa, scroll through my phone and wait for him to come home. When he hit me, I made sure Ariana didn't see. I started to realise, I was sinking.

Daniel kicked me down the stairs. I went into labour. The doctors worked on my baby for twenty minutes, trying to get her to breathe. Eventually they found an airway and I heard my little girl cry. I knew for my children I had to build up the confidence and get out. I had to stop us sinking.

One morning I was walking to the shops, when Daniel followed me. I ran to the till and said, 'Call the police, I need to get away from him, get me out, get me out.'

I remember being in the back of the shop, shaking with my children. I had to pull us out. I had to pull us out or we were all going to sink.

19: I'M YOUR MATCH

We met in October. By Valentine's Day we'd moved in. It was mad and risky, yeah. But in life, I'd rather do things than not.

We'd not been together long when Stephen got ill. Pain, passing blood, things like that. He got the diagnosis – polycystic kidney disease.

We didn't know how long he'd got. Stephen's one of those people, he just cracks on, he just wanted to carry on living, see what happened. He never considered looking for a donor.

His kidney function got worse and worse and before long, it was very low. The hospital kept giving him these packs, to apply for a living donor. They must have given him at least four, but he'd just put them away somewhere. Me and his mum, we were saying, 'Stephen, let us get tested.' He just said no.

My car had gone in for an MOT, so I took Stephen's car to work. I parked up and still to this day I don't know why I did this – I opened his glove box. There was the living donor pack.

I didn't think twice. I sat in the car, filled it out, posted it off.

I didn't tell Stephen I'd done it until they rang me up. They asked me to go in for tests. Stephen said no. He said, 'I can't let you risk your life for me.' But I was like, well sort of, I just was like, shut up, basically. I'm doing it.

I had this feeling, all the way through. I just kept telling him, 'I'm your match. I just know it. I'm your match.' And well, guess what. I'm always right.

I hadn't realised how yellow his eyes had gone until my kidney was in him and they turned back to their normal colour. If we'd have been much later, waited much longer, well I don't know if Stephen would be here.

All my life, I'd been walking around with this kidney, my kidney, that was also his kidney. His exact match. I'd been his match for all my life and we didn't even know.

We'd met in October and moved in on Valentine's Day and this February will mark nineteen years living together. It's been mad and risky, yeah. But in life, I'd rather do things than not.

20: SNOW

My wife thought I was ridiculous. But I had to get there. I had to get to work. I was determined that if my patients could get there, someone would be there to see them.

It was snowing a lot when we went to bed. When I woke up at half past four, it was snowing even more. Completely impassable.

Put my work clothes in my backpack, put thermals on underneath and waterproofs on top.

It was pitch black and chucking it down with snow. The way I cycle to work is the Pennine Trail – Barnsley to Sheffield. Twenty kilometres. It's rural woodland mostly. There was no way I was getting a bike through. I started to walk.

At first, I was literally up to my waist. I wade through, swim through the snow, and the sun starts to rise. The trees get taller and taller the further in you go. The sunlight dapples through the leaves.

Silence. Total peace and total silence. And as I walk in the silence I realise, wow, in life, with our phones and work and everything, how busy and noisy the world is. We never have silence, not truly, but here it is. Here I am in it.

I thought about my wife and she was right, it was ridiculous. But all of us do ridiculous, extraordinary things all the time. Very ill patients find the will and the strength to volunteer. Other NHS workers doing anything and everything they can for their patients. I subscribe to the idea that people are basically good. That it's part of our nature, nature, to help each other. It's human.

Three and a half hours later and I get into Sheffield. Change into my work clothes. Out of the silence. Back into the noise.

25: ANYONE CAN WIN

Strength.

At twenty-five my body started to break down. Twenty years of playing rugby it was like, enough. Enough. Stop.

Balance.

I've always played sport. Even though you wouldn't know it to look at me, I'm a big guy, I've always done it, so I couldn't just stop. I needed something else. Something else. But what?

Charge.

I'd always assumed sumo was just two fat lads running into each other. But it's so much more than that.

Strength.

I love it when the big guys come in and they think they're gonna walk all over everyone. It's never that simple. We have weight categories so we can have big guys against big guys. But we do also do open weight, so if you're small and you really want to take on a giant, you can.

Balance.

You look at the big guy and the small guy and you think, the big guy's gonna walk it. No question. But when the small guy has speed, technicality, if they manage to put the big guy off balance, get him to trip over his own feet, he can win.

Charge.

The rules are incredibly simple. You fight in a circular ring, four and a half metres across. You win by pushing your opponent out of it, or making anything other than the soles of their feet touch the floor. That's it. Those are the rules.

So, so simple, right? But it takes a lifetime to master. That's the beauty. Those simple rules mean that every single person, every individual, is so unique. In theory you're doing the same thing but in practice you've found your complete individual own way of mastering it. And anyone can win, if they find their own way.

Strength. Balance. Charge.

27: THE LEMON TREE

At our drop-in we're open five nights a week. We try to keep homeless people alive.

In the early days, we served ex-miners, people left over from the strike. A few years before they were underground, risking their lives.

We've had pregnant women and children queuing up outside. Kids who've had enough and run away from home.

Everyone knows Joe, he's been coming to us since forever. He kicks around the town centre, outside the Lemon Tree.

One girl, she comes in and she locks herself in the toilet. Just to be a bit naughty, for a bit of a laugh.

I've only had one occasion where a client hit a volunteer and I don't like saying it, but the volunteer probably deserved it. They said things you shouldn't say to a person who is homeless.

We feed a couple of bouncers, who used to work the doors in Barnsley. Got themselves into trouble with drinking, lost everything.

Everyone knows Joe, he's been coming to us since forever. One day he disappeared from outside the Lemon Tree. We didn't see him at the drop-in after that.

We found one lad in town, a child really. He'd run away from his mum's new partner and spent two weeks living on the roof of Boots.

One client started shoplifting. Their begging money dried up. Nobody carries cash, so they had to try their luck.

It's hard when a client stops coming. Have they gone to prison? Died? Or just moved on? You worry where that person could be.

I was hiking with my brother, out Dodworth way. I was walking past a bungalow when I heard somebody shout my name. I turned around and saw it was Joe. Joe from outside the Lemon Tree. Inside his bungalow, he'd put carpets down, his garden was all manicured, everything like that. He'd made it.

At our drop-in we're open five nights a week. We try to keep homeless people alive. We've twenty boxes and seven crates full of tea, coffee, biscuits, handwarmers, foil blankets, all sorts. When you give an item out, you say something without using any words:

'You are loved, things can get better. I love the person you are and believe in the person you can be. You can make it.'

28: WE ALL DESERVE TO BE CARED FOR

We all deserve to be cared for.

I decided to join the police at two years old. There were officers walking down our street and I loved the uniform. So that was that.

On the streets in the eighties it could get pretty rough. And I had a habit of, if I came across trouble, taking it on head first. It was my grandma who said, 'You carry on doing what you're doing Amanda, you're gonna end up in a wheelchair.'

A few months later I ended up in a fight with a man who was high on drugs. He'd been released from an institution when he absolutely shouldn't have been. It wasn't his fault. I left the scene with multiple back injuries and had to retire from the police at twenty-eight.

It was like the biggest chunk of my life had been taken away. The things I wanted to do, just, no longer possible. I became invisible.

We all deserve to be cared for.

My dog Jupiter, he was like a little teddy bear. Only six weeks old. I taught him how to walk next to my wheelchair. Basic manners. And then we got accepted on this support dog programme and honestly, what they taught him to do next – it's crazy.

They taught him to take my socks off, load and unload the washing machine, get me a chair, call the lift, take off my coat.

At the start, I thought I wasn't going to be able to do the things I used to. He's turned me back into me. In fact, he's made me even better.

We all deserve to be cared for.

I've done a 10K. I've climbed Snowdon. I've gone from being invisible to getting to know the whole community – and they've all fallen in love with Jupiter.

It was really sudden. Exactly like it'd been with me. One day, without any warning, Jupiter's legs stopped working. He had to retire there and then.

I have a new support dog now, but Jupiter's still here with us. I care for him – the way he cared for me. I want to give him the best life possible. Because no matter what happens, what life throws your way – we all deserve to be cared for.

29: WRONG CROWD

I got in the wrong crowd as a teenager.

I took speed at school. I put it in a Rizla and just swallowed it. I thought to myself, 'Oh, this isn't even working,' but all of a sudden, I felt this buzz from my feet all the way to the top of my head.

Be loyal to your mates, don't feel your emotions and get wrecked whenever, wherever. That's what I thought it meant to be a man. It's like I was on this path of destruction.

A couple of days after Christmas, I got really drunk, really high and thought it would be a good idea to jump out of the window of my mate's three-storey flat. The hospital discharged me on New Year's Eve with a broken back and a Zimmer frame. So, what did I do? I went back to my mates, drank a pint of vodka and snorted a big bag of cocaine.

I'd be at home with my girlfriend, and I would feel totally fine but then I'd go to the shop for a loaf of bread and not come home. I'd bump into somebody and then I'd go to the next house and then to the next house, until I realised I'd been gone for five days.

It got to the point of taking ecstasy tablets, one after the other after the other after the other. It's not that I wanted to die in those moments. I just hated myself, I felt like crap. I had this mentality that, 'I'm the man, I'm gonna live forever, no drug is gonna defeat me.'

The cycle broke when I walked into the welcome area of a church. Somebody came over and said 'Good morning' and I just burst into floods of tears. That was on a Sunday and I was crying on and off until Tuesday. It was like this deep-rooted pain in my heart just started to lift and heal.

I got in the wrong crowd as a teenager and I was led down a path where I was an addict for fourteen years. Next year, I'll be fifteen years clean. I've a wife, three sons and a daughter now. I'm not in the wrong crowd anymore.

30: ACORNS

A saying runs in my family – 'From little acorns do mighty oak trees grow.'

I was a single parent with two children and I had a full-time job in palliative care. I found this lump and it grew and grew and grew. Life gives you whispers. And if you ignore them, life gives you bigger whispers, doesn't it? All of a sudden, I was sat next to my patients in the waiting room.

I did my chemo, did my radiotherapy and got discharged from the hospital. Sitting at home, that was when I crumbled. Everybody else's world kept spinning but mine had totally stopped. I couldn't go back to work. I couldn't face it. But then this little acorn of an idea started to grow in me.

I'd procrastinated before about starting a choir. But now I thought, 'Stop messing about and do it.' We started small but now, we've thirty ladies and one man who come. We've all faced the loneliness of cancer. We don't read music and people sometimes get the words wrong or come in at the wrong time. But when we all sing together, we make something beautiful. You should hear our 'Super Trouper', honestly, it's fabulous.

The choir were there on my wedding day, singing on the Town Hall steps. We booked it for August and there wasn't a cloud in the sky. By then, I'd been given the all clear, I was deemed cured. But with cancer you're never cured, it's always at the back of your mind that it might come back. When we sing, I forget.

That day my son gave me this necklace. It had an acorn on it. He said, 'This acorn is your marriage, Mum. From little acorns do mighty oak trees grow.'

38: COMER-INNER

I first heard the term at the local shop – 'comer-inner'. I'd just moved here and needed milk and bread. The woman behind the counter took one look at me and said, 'Well, who are you then? You're not from here, are you?'

That's the thing in Barnsley – if your face is new, it sticks out.

In that corner shop I remembered – I'd been a comer-inner once before. When I was a child my parents moved us from one town to another, when they couldn't afford to keep their farm. In the playground I was punched and kicked and teased for speaking different, acting different, not knowing the games.

I'd not known there was a term for it, but I was a comer-inner back then, and here I was – a comer-inner all over again.

And I understand it. People here have shared history. They worked together in the steelworks, the pits, the pipeworks. They've taken the same holidays, they've played in the same fields.

They belong – not just to a place, but to each other.

Years after moving here, when I had kids and was dropping them at the school gates, it was still the same question, 'Who are you, then?' Not unkind, necessarily. Just – not included.

It hasn't mattered how long I've lived here – two years, twelve years, twenty years. I'll always be a comer-inner.

But we've stayed. We've been here thirty-eight years now. Made friends – mostly other comer-inners. Found our own patch. Forged our own space. Found our own way of belonging to a place and to each other.

Now, my children have grown up here. And I've always tried to teach them, you know, that it's okay for people to arrive. It's okay for people to be new.

We don't always lose something by opening the door. Maybe sometimes we even gain something – when we let people come in.

40: ROUND AND ROUND

I walk through that car park every Thursday night when I'm going for my chippy tea. I go late to avoid the queues, the crush, and in the hope they might give us some scraps – they normally do for the last man standing.

During the day that car park is rammed, absolutely chock-a-block. It's Armageddon, it's Black Friday, it's Hunger Games trying to get a space. At night I could dance through that car park naked and no one – not a sausage – would know except for me and the stars.

It was a while ago. My normal Thursday night, walking through that car park, but this time it wasn't empty. There was a car. Just one, lights on, engine on, two boys sat in the front.

The next Thursday there were two cars. And every week after that it just kept on growing. Three, four, five cars. Lights on, engines on, two boys sat in the front.

Sometimes the cars were parked far away from each other. Sometimes they were right up close, windows down, boys leaning out, having a chat.

Sometimes they'd be driving, doing doughnuts, screeching their wheels. All that energy and speed, all that grandstanding and posturing, acting like Billy Big Bollocks, but really – they're just little boys going round and round in circles.

Every Thursday I was trying to watch what they were doing, trying to work out why they were there. Sometimes I'd get home and my chips would be stone cold.

One night I had enough. I started walking, power walking, towards one of the cars. I must have spooked them, because this car, it went nought to a hundred in about three seconds. It screeched away from me like a scared little pussycat. Not all the way out the car park mind, just to park up at the other end.

And that's when something clicked for me. He didn't leave all the way. Because he didn't have anywhere else to go. That's what they're doing there. Just existing.

I still walk through that car park every Thursday night but now as I pass, I give the boys a nod and they nod back. No, I don't mind them being there anymore. But I do hope one day there's more to their lives than going round and round in circles.

44: IT'S GONNA RAIN

My husband must have about five different weather apps on his phone. It's been a dry year, absolutely no rain to speak of. David constantly just looks at his apps and he says the same thing.

'It's gonna rain, it's gonna rain, it's gonna rain.'

When David's grandfather owned the farm, they did everything. Pigs, sheep, potatoes, chickens, milk rounds. You name it, they did it. The farm had so many hands, it even had its own football team.

'It's gonna rain.'

Back then there were forty-four staff on the farm, now there's just three family. We do it all. Sowing the seed, feed, weed, disease control, harvesting, drying, storing.

'It's gonna rain.'

In times of drought when the weatherman says, 'It's going to rain,' people get upset and say, 'But I want to sit in my garden.' I can't help but think, 'Yeah, but do you want to eat?'

'It's gonna rain.'

A few years ago it really rained. So much, we flooded out. The water was so high, you could only see the top of the wheat. When the flood went down, the crop was just filthy. When the land dried out, we found dead fish in the tramlines of the field.

'It's gonna rain.'

I'm just hoping for an average year. No more floods, no more drought, no more sitting in the office till two in the morning worrying if we'll harvest enough grain.

'It's gonna rain.'

In the barn, I stand by the window and look out over the fields. I think of all the generations who were here before me and what they gave to the farm and this land. Will my children and my children's children be able to do the same?

'It's gonna rain, it's gonna rain, it's gonna rain.'

46: THE STINK

When we first moved to where we still live now, we had septic tanks. Big, round concrete bunkers, covered with wood over the top. But there was no covering them up, really – they were giant pits of poo.

All of our neighbours' poo, it would all drain into the septic tanks at the end of our garden. That's how it goes. Sometimes in life you end up at the bottom of the hill, with everyone else's poo on your doorstep.

The tanks, non-stop, would get blocked. Blocked. And then blocked again. I knew it had got bad when I was in the shops. I told someone where I live, number forty-six, and they said, 'Oh I know it! Smelly corner!'

Roger, who lived in the house behind us, became a man obsessed. A poo vigilante. Every day, rain or shine, he'd walk down our path with his dog Ruby and check the tanks. He'd lift the manhole, peer in, see what was blocking the pipes and try to fish it out.

Lynsey was the worst culprit. Every year at Christmas she'd make a Christmas cake, mess it up, flush it down. It always, always blocked the tanks. So every year, there we were, having to rod it out – with this big wiry contraption, like a medieval toilet brush.

Eventually, the council made us rip the septic tanks out. The Environmental Agency got wind that our poo was actually pouring into the stream nearby. Turns out, it was getting into the water supply.

They said we had to come together, all the neighbours, to get rid of the tanks. So out we came, everyone. Even Lynsey turned up with her sledgehammer. It felt poetic: her cake blocked the system; her hammer smashed it up.

You don't really know a place until you've rodded poo out of a twelve-foot pit with your neighbours. It's disgusting. It's bonding. And it teaches you – sometimes you inherit problems you didn't create. But what matters is how you deal with the stink – together.

50: THE FACE OF BARNSLEY

The *Barnsley Chronicle* was always in the middle of our kitchen table. My dad would say fifty pence is an absolute bargain for so many nutty headlines, football results and obituaries.

I'll never forget the day I came down for breakfast and there it was, on the kitchen table, on the front of the *Chron* in massive letters: 'Could YOU be the Face of Barnsley?'

A ticket to stardom – a catwalk at the Metrodome, maybe a modelling contract if you were lucky. All you had to do was send in a photo. They'd print them all side by side and let the public vote.

When the next *Chron* landed on the kitchen table I flipped straight to the men's section to check out the competition.

It looked like a police line-up. Mugshot city. I mean, honestly. It was less *GQ* and more like Britain's Most Wanted.

I was fifteen. Just old enough to start thinking I was someone. I didn't enter. But in my head? I could have won. Still, I voted. I judged. I laughed. I thought, who do these guys think they are?

I imagined my face among theirs. I imagined beating them all, winning, and becoming the face of my town.

I never had the guts to send a photo in.

I suppose, deep down, it's cos I didn't want people to laugh at me. The way I laughed at them. It's easier to judge others than to look inwards, isn't it?

The Face of Barnsley is gone now. COVID probably finished it off, like it did most things. But I still think about those faces sometimes. I envy them. It was never about beauty. It was about belonging. Those men? They were brave, in a way. They said, 'Here I am.'

I hid.

We might not be the sexiest bunch. But we are the faces of Barnsley.

And that's enough.

55: THE PULL

When I passed my driving test, I felt a weight lift. No more parents, no more trains, no more buses. I could go where I want, when I want. I was finally free.

My father had this old car that was always breaking down. The suspension was dodgy, the fluid system leaked, so naturally he passed it on to me. He didn't bother where I took it, as long as he knew I had a map on the passenger seat.

Every Friday night, I'd get in the car with no idea where I was going. North, south, east or west, it didn't matter. I'd turn on the radio, hit the road and wind up staying in a pub somewhere.

My father had a sister who lived on a farm. One weekend I drove down to her and we got talking about our family tree. She showed me some photographs of my great-grandfather, a face I'd never seen. She told me where he was buried and all of a sudden, I had this pull inside me.

I drove to Gloucester, found the church, and told the vicar who I was. He shouted for a very old lady who knew where to look. We went outside and found my great-grandfather's grave, covered in ivy.

I wasn't expecting it, but I left that graveyard wanting to follow the next link and the next link to see where it would lead. So, I carried on tracing my family tree.

I've looked through parish records, marriage certificates and gravestones online. I did a DNA test that suggests my family was here before Roman times in 55 BC.

I've driven round the country and learnt the chaos of life. My existence is a series of marriages, deaths, battles, accidents, near misses, wars and tragedies.

When I passed my driving test, I felt a weight lift. No more parents, no more trains, no more buses. I could go where I want, when I want. I was finally free. Turns out the road was pulling me home. Back to my family.

57: CARDBOARD BOX

You're not supposed to have favourites, but Martin was my favourite brother. When we were kids, we'd go down into the village and he'd push me on my go-kart, or on my little bike. He'd go around nicking people's milk money off their doorstep. We used to go everywhere together. I'd never let my brother leave my side.

Martin was fifty-seven when he went missing. He was in and out of prison a lot, so you'd have times when he'd just disappear. I got a letter through the door. It was from the police saying, 'Can you get in touch with us? We need to talk to you.'

Two kids had gone to visit their grandma and grandad for the weekend. They'd been out playing football in this field when they found a skull. It was all over the news. Police went round thousands of houses, knocking on doors. Asking if anybody knew anything or had seen anything.

The police concluded their investigations. They said it was murder. They said the body was Martin.

At the morgue, the coroner showed me a photo of my brother's body – his torso and his arms were missing. They said, 'Do you want to go inside this room and see him now?' and I said, 'Yes, he's my brother.'

I goes into this little room, white walls and I see Martin's skeleton on this table all laid out. That was when it hit me. I got hold of his skull, I was bawling my eyes out and I wouldn't let go. All his remains were put in a cardboard box and given to me.

I dream about it – what happened to my brother. Same dream, all the time.

I see him stood in a field, with a cottage in the distance. I see two men shoot him, drag him and bury him under these conifers. Then it snows, then it rains. I see a tractor, ploughing the field and driving over his bones. I see foxes and badgers come in and take bits of Martin away.

I haven't had a funeral for my brother. I keep him, still in the cardboard box, at the bottom of my bed. When I die, he'll be buried with me. We used to go everywhere together. I'm never letting my brother leave my side again.

60: LIVING WELL

It's not about death and dying. It's about living and living well.

There can sometimes be slight resistance, when people are first referred here. They don't want to give up, they want to fight. But we show them round and say you know, 'Look – there's sounds of music and smells of home-made cooking. There's people having coffee together and here's our beautiful garden.'

It's a place of life.

And we make sure – things don't happen to the patient, but with the patient. I honestly couldn't be a nurse anywhere else.

There was a couple where they had a significant anniversary coming up but they knew they weren't going to make it. When they were young and courting they loved going to the cinema together. We couldn't get them to the cinema, so we brought the cinema to them. Set up a screen, got popcorn, and nice lights. Just like when they were teenagers.

One patient wished to see his horse one last time. So we worked with his family and friends to bring it here. Not inside obviously, in the car park. The patient was took out to see his horse and it created such a buzz. The kitchen staff came out with carrots, all the other patients came out too.

I had a patient who was the same age as me with children the same age as my children. The morning that her little boys had come to say goodbye, I did have to take a minute to step out. You see lots of hard things, but as a nurse you want to know you've done your best for the whole journey.

I gathered my thoughts, composed myself, and sixty seconds later, stepped back in.

Like any hospice, you have to be from the area to get referred. If this place didn't exist then Barnsley just wouldn't get hospice care. And the people of Barnsley deserve memories and comfort and love. Because this place – it's not about death and dying. It's about living and living well.

68: REGULAR SPOT

When my grandma died, my grandad had a lot of family. There was always one of us checking in, popping in, going round. Then he started going to Spoons where he had his regular spot by the window – table sixty-eight.

The days when he wasn't seeing family or going to Spoons, I started to notice something. The night before he would go to bed very, very late. And then that morning – the mornings when he had no plans – he just wouldn't get out of bed.

He didn't show his emotions, my grandad. So it took me a while to realise. On those days, he wasn't getting up because he didn't have anyone to get up for.

I'd meet older people who were just like my grandad in lots of ways. But with no family checking in, popping in, going round. I thought about the days when my grandad wouldn't have those things – the days he wouldn't get out of bed. That was some people's every day. I got a job running social clubs.

The more I put on, the more people came. The job grew. I started pairing people up. Younger people who would go round to an older person's house, an hour a week, have a cuppa, a chat, a laugh. Someone local who would become a friend for life. Someone to get out of bed for.

I never wanted to think about growing old. But now, meeting older people, I think yeah, I want to get older like you. I want to try to stay connected, social, have a regular spot by the window. Ask for help when I need it.

When my grandad died we knew he'd had a good innings. And he'd spent his time with people. Because that's the bottom line – people need people. And we all deserve someone to get out of bed for.

70: BERNARD'S WATCH

Bernard's Watch was a children's TV show many moons ago. Where this kid, Bernard, had a pocket watch that when he clicked it, everybody froze apart from him.

I've always thought Barnsley's like that. Time moves forward for me but everyone and everything in Barnsley seems to stay the same.

I loved growing up in Worsbrough. Fields, fresh air, freedom. I think we were the last generation not trapped by mobile phones. I could run off out with friends and my parents didn't know where I was.

When I moved to Manchester, every time I'd come back on weekends, I'd see the town a little bit different. Like *Bernard's Watch*, so much had happened to me, but everything here wor the same.

I realised, everybody knew everybody. If I smoked in Barnsley, if one person saw me, that wor it. It'd get straight back to my mum and dad. At home my mum was like, 'No pictures on the walls, no photos, no posts.' In Manchester, I could smoke. I had my own room and it was mine and I could put up any stuff I wanted.

It got to the point where, when I'd come back to Barnsley, I just didn't want to see anyone or talk to anyone. I'd make excuses, avoid people and then, slowly, gradually, I stopped coming back at all.

After uni I moved to London. I wor living in a five-bedroom house share, with the landlord smoking weed up in the attic and my housemates smoking weed downstairs. And I started reading this book. It was about time. How we spend our time. And I realised, reading this book – my parents are seventy. If I see them once a year and they live until they're eighty, I'll only see them ten more times.

One day I was at a station in London, about to get the tube back to my weed-smelling house share, and I saw one of the trains departing was going to Sheffield. And I thought, 'I'm gonna get on it. I've got stuff at home. I'm just gonna get on that train and go back.'

When I got there, I was sat in the garden, sat with my family and I just knew – I don't want to go back down. There was no part of me that wanted to go back down to London.

You can't stop people from getting older. Things might feel like they stay the same – but turns out, it's only Bernard who can actually stop time.

73: STILL DANCING

Christmas at the Londoner, that's where I met him.

My mother never encouraged me to do education. No books. I had two brothers, they were encouraged, yeah, but not me.

I left school at fifteen. If I wanted any money to go out with, I had to go and earn it. I got a job at the Co-op chemist. The pay was only two fifty a week. So I also worked on market on a Saturday, selling material. That wor worth every bit of time – I got about another quid for doing that. After we'd finished on market we used to go, 'Ah come, come on, on t' pub.'

I used to go out seven days a week, believe it or not. A lot of us underage, as they did in them days. There was something to do every single night of the week. Them were the days.

Monday it was Ponderosa. Tuesday Cutting Edge. Wednesday New Lodge. Thursday Cutting Edge again. Monk Bretton Social on Friday. Wakefield Theatre Club on a Saturday. And then Sunday, into town, all the pubs down there – King George, Bodega, the lot. We loved it. We loved going out.

But the best nightclub in town – the Londoner. Oh we would dance. What a time. It wor fantastic.

Christmas at the Londoner that's where I met him. My husband. We met there and we've never looked back. I'm seventy-three now and we're still dancing. Not every night of the week anymore. But not far off.

75: FLAGS AND BANNERS

When I was a lad, I listened to alternative music. Music that was different. Music that challenged the mainstream. Growing up in a mining community, the music I listened to was socialist, the meetings I went to were socialist, so there was only one thing I was going to be.

During the strike, I was there at the front of the picket line, I was there at the Battle of Orgreave, I was there when we marched behind the pit band and banner when the strike was called off.

This Miners' Hall looks like a church, with its stained glass windows and pulpit at the front. When I come in here, I can still see the pit delegates debating and the union officials standing there, shouting and bawling.

There's a photograph somewhere of this hall full of tins, donated by trade unions from all over the world. Back in the strike we had no wages, but supporters would donate plenty of snap. The labels on the tins from the Soviets was hard to fathom. My mate accidentally ate some dog meat. Apparently it went lovely with a tin of soup.

Round the hall are banners that each colliery paraded at political rallies and galas. Painted on them are messages of camaraderie and hope. Health, peace, safety at work, dignity for all races. I remember marching under these banners. They're things we're still fighting for today.

Talk these days is less about banners and more about flags. One went up near my house the other day. I know some miners who've been conned by the far right. It's not about nationalism, it's about class. Some people seem to have forgotten their history.

A guy recently told me the lifespan of a banner is seventy-five years. You can see the tears in the fabric, the frays on the edges. On one of our banners, there's a clenched fist. I can see it disintegrating away.

When school groups visit our hall, I tell them, 'I've never met kings or queens, but I've met a lot of miners and I know whose company I'd rather keep.' I've never been a fan of flags myself. What have kings and queens and their flags ever done for Barnsley, ever done for miners, ever done for the likes of you and me?

79: A MOMENT TOGETHER

Drag my case – my suitcase with all my kit in it.

The first time you do it you feel so weird. Like, 'What, I'm just gonna stand on the street and start singing?' I was sixteen and me and my sister went outside, I took my guitar and we sang.

I've had loads of different jobs. I've been a teacher, a cleaner, I've worked in a cafe. When my son was born, I stayed at home with him. Then COVID hit.

A suitcase with all my kit in it – I arrive and claim my spot.

During lockdown I picked up my guitar again and started singing. Two weeks later, I braved outside. I set up next to Poundland and I thought, 'Let's just do it.'

I claim my spot – set up the microphone stand. Tablet, lyrics, livestream.

Now, I know so many people by name, they come over, we have a little chat and then we sing.

There's Mary who's got dementia. She sometimes forgets why she's come into town but she'll always remember the words to the songs.

Then there's Alan, he's seventy-nine. He used to sing round the karaoke places in town. When we first sang 'Sweet Caroline' together this crowd gathered. They were all dancing and clapping along. It was so overwhelming at the end I was like, 'Thank you, Barnsley!' It was like I was headlining Wembley.

Tablet, lyrics, livestream. Plug in and I'm ready to go.

When you busk, whatever people are going through, they stop to share a moment with you. It's not about showing off, or my voice. It's about a moment together. And then it's gone.

Another day done. Unplug, pack down, leave my spot. Drag my case home – my suitcase with all my kit in it.

93: PAVILION

When we were young lads, fifteen-year-old kids, my best mate Parky and me would sit on top of the pavilion at Barnsley Cricket Club. One night after practice, Parky turned to me and said, 'I wonder what life holds for you and me?'

'Don't go in nightclubs, don't gamble, don't smoke, don't drink, go to church on a Sunday. You are not going down a mine, you're not having that for a life.' That wor the advice father drilled into me.

Mother used to fill this tin bath by the fire. When he finished his shift down the pit, father'd come home, and I'd watch the water turn black. Father was up at half past four but after work he always made sure we went into this little park to practise, practise, practise cricket.

I gave my life to the game and in return it gave me a chance to see the world. I never married. I got myself married to cricket. Every time I stepped onto the field, I took a breath and said, 'I'm going to enjoy this.'

Through all the years, thick and thin, Parky stayed close to me. On my telly I watched his chat show and saw that boy from Barnsley rise to the top.

It wor a Wednesday night when he rung me up. We cracked a few jokes, had a few tears in our eyes and I had this feeling we wouldn't see each other again. We said goodbye, and that was it. On Thursday morning, he'd gone.

On Church Lane, where I was born, there was a row of old houses. Now on that exact spot, ninety-three years on, there's a statue of me. I've stood there many a time and shed many a tear.

I think of those young lads on top of the pavilion. Born in hard times, but who would have known what joy life held for Parky and me?

100: GET THEM OFF THE BOOKS

Every morning there was a queue outside the door. At the job centre we saw hundreds a day. You weren't supposed to have feelings, no. You were supposed to coerce them, manipulate them, do whatever to tick the boxes and get them off the books.

This one woman I worked with, she'd come to work with a gold necklace, bangles, rings, the lot. We always dressed down because we were working with the unemployed and honestly you could see the query on people's faces. She'd sit across from ex-miners, telling them what to do, just dripping in gold. I mean honestly.

Upstairs in a cubicle, I'd listen to the nuts and kernels of conversation, collecting clues on what jobs these men could do. I filled in so many forms for so many men who'd been to the bowels and confines of the earth but couldn't read or write. They'd make excuses like 'I've forgotten my glasses' and things like that.

I had so many men break in front of me. This one guy, thirty-odd, strong bloke, I can see him now. He was just missing his workmates, the brotherhood, the camaraderie, going down the pits and putting his life in the hands of the man working next to him. Like so many, he was asking, 'Can you do anything for me, lass? Is there actually anything you can do?'

The thing about the men sitting across from me was they'd say 'All I can do is work down the pit' but they wanted a life above it. They wanted jobs out in nature, jobs driving out on the open road, jobs where they could fly free.

At the end of the day, I'd sit there exhausted. I didn't talk to my colleagues about it. The ones dripping in gold, sitting at the back drinking tea.

It was like we had hundreds and hundreds and hundreds of men on this conveyor belt. Where's the humanity? The caring touch? I thought it was people we were dealing with.

101: THE CYCLE CONTINUES

If Barnsley Council is famous for something, it's the one hundred and one ways they can get out of answering a question. I'm convinced their catchphrase is 'Don't get me involved'. For years and years, I've been stuck.

I call the council, they ghost me, the cycle continues.

On the recreation ground, a stone's throw away from my house, the miners built a pavilion. It wor made out of wood, a bit like an army camp, and it was everything the community required. Galas, football matches, raffles, tombolas, best baby competitions – you name it.

I call the council.

When the pavilion went up in flames, the heart of our village went with it. I pass people on the street and I don't know who they are. Back in the day, miners used to spend their money in the local shop, the local baker, the local butchers. Now we've only got a pub and that must be on its last legs. I am determined to rebuild the pavilion and bring our community back.

They ghost me.

I've always been somebody who'll take on an impossible challenge. We've lost seven people in the years we've been campaigning. All of them totally behind the pavilion. They've died, gone. I am not letting this go.

The cycle continues.

I've organised fundraisers, conducted feasibility studies, answered parish surveys, voted in local parish polls, researched community asset transfers, written a business plan, visited the archives, spoken to my local MP, I've even rung up the Chief Fire Officer for South Yorkshire. What else am I supposed to do?

I call the council, they ghost me, the cycle continues.

103: LITTLE RITUALS

I recently moved into a house without any curtains, and I have this little ritual that I do at the end of every day. I go upstairs, stick my head out the bedroom window and wait for someone's bathroom light to come on. When I hear a toilet flush, that's when I can go to bed.

I've counted one hundred and three houses on my street, but there is one window that has caught my eye. There's a guy with a mane of blond hair who has become my obsession. If I see his bathroom light come on, I can't resist. Every night he sits on the toilet for fifteen minutes without fail.

I think there's a reason he stays on the toilet so long. He lives in a busy house. Lots of people, dogs and things. I think he goes there for a bit of time on his own. In this small moment of intimacy, I can see him, but he can't see me.

I never thought much of it until one day, quite recently. I was in Iceland doing the shop when I saw this flash of blond in one of the aisles and there he was, just standing there. I looked at him and he looked at me. I opened my mouth to say hello and suddenly remembered, he didn't actually know me.

As he bent down to get his peas and made his way towards the checkout, I thought, 'I wonder what you're going to eat those peas with tonight? I'll watch you poo that out later.' And sure enough, that night I saw his bathroom light turn on and I heard his toilet flush.

150: THREE GREGGS, ONE TOWN

Did you know there are three Greggs in Barnsley Town Centre? You can walk from the first to the second to the third in less than eight minutes. Yeah, you can – trust me, I've timed it.

You can get breakfast in one, dinner in second, tea in third. Or, if it's more your style: starter, main, pudding. I tend to go for – Greggs One. Sausage roll. Greggs Two. Steak bake. Greggs Three. Yum Yum. Job's a good'un.

There's always queues coming out all three of them, right out the doors. Getting this town their pasties and pastries is Barnsley's equivalent to the emergency services. But the staff are always so calm and kind and if they ever run out of anything, you can trust that the oven is on and it won't be long until the next batch is ready.

I saw this young guy in town wearing a Greggs tracksuit and I had to ask him, I said, 'Where d'ya get that?' He said, 'Primark! They've partnered up with Greggs and they're selling merch.' He said he just had to buy it, he loved Greggs that much. 'My mum,' he said. 'She wor a single mum and there was five of us, and Greggs wor the place that could fill up the whole family for less than a tenner. Where else can you say does that?'

When I wor a kid we weren't rich but we never struggled for food. There were places you could go, veg wor cheap, and you had community cafes where you could get nutritious hot meals for next to nothing. No wonder the queues are out the door and round the corner. No wonder this town needs three Greggs, eight minutes apart. Supply and demand.

230: FUNERAL GEAR

What happened was, my friend's dad died. Anne rung me up at work, I was in a job at a curtain shop at the time, and I said, 'Oh, I'll definitely come to the funeral. Two o'clock, I'll see you there.'

The day arrives, so I gets my funeral gear on – a blouse, dark jacket, trousers and that – and off I go to the crematorium.

Now they're a massive family, these Fletchers, absolutely massive. Aunties, uncles, seven or eight grandkids and God knows what. So I move past the crowd and think, 'I'll go in and sit at the back.'

They start to come in with the coffin and I look at the faces. And I don't recognise anyone. The aunties aren't there. The uncles aren't there. The grandkids aren't there. Anne's not there. Oh my God, whose funeral is this?

They shut the doors and that was it, you can't very well go knocking saying 'Let me out, let me out' so I thought, right then, Patricia. Head down, best get on with it.

All through the service, I could hear people whispering, 'Whose that lass sat at the back?' and, 'I think she worked at the corner shop near our John,' and I'm thinking, 'Don't talk to me, don't talk to me, don't talk to me.'

I must say though, he sounded like a lovely man this John Williams. I wish I'd met him when he was alive.

As soon as they'd done 'Abide with Me' and the service was over, I put some money in the collection and I was out of there quick. As I'm leaving this fella says, 'Oh, it's lovely for you to come,' and I say, 'Well, I've got to shoot off, I've got to get back to work,' and I go hide behind this tree.

And I'm stood there thinking, 'Oh my God, what am I going to do?' when a hearse turns the corner. I see aunts, uncles, seven or eight grandkids, Anne. Turns out the funeral was at half past two.

I dusted myself off, came out from behind the tree and walked back, back into the church. The guy on the door said, 'Haven't you just been in, love?' I said, 'Yes,' and I sat back down.

300: THE FREEDOM RIDERS

I'll never forget when I was teaching in the eighties. The head brought the police into school to do a session with the kids. In the assembly a young lad stuck his hand up and asked, 'What do police do with those big truncheons?' And the answer was, 'We're very careful how we use them.' Meanwhile, on the picket line, the police were using them to bludgeon miners in the face.

When I retired, I got in the routine of getting the train to go and see my granddaughter in Leeds. With my elderly pass, I was able to travel for free and take the youngster far and wide. The powers that be decided to do away with the elderly travel pass.

A group of us, all pensioners, decided to call a meeting in the old library. We spent all week leafleting train and bus stations. I expected a reasonable turnout, but I couldn't believe it when over three hundred people turned up.

In the coming days, we spent a lot of time discussing it until someone said, 'Back in the day, civil rights activists used to have freedom rides in the United States. Why don't we do the same?' A few were saying, 'We can't get on the train and not pay. We'll be breaking the law!' So, we took a vote, and the majority said, 'Let's go for it.'

We all turned up at Barnsley Interchange for our first action. We put out a message to pensioners from Doncaster, Rotherham and Sheffield to freedom ride to Meadowhall. When we got on the platform, there was a very nice guy from Northern Rail who said, 'Don't worry, there's been some confusion. We'll let you use your passes today.'

We did the same action every Monday for four weeks, until we were stopped in our tracks by a load of British Transport Police. We were stuck, until someone said, 'Look, we can't get onto this platform, but there's no one guarding the platform on the other side!'

We legged it out the waiting room, over the footbridge and jumped on a train. I'll never forget the aghast look on the face of the British Transport Police, still on the other side of the platform, as the train pulled away and we waved them goodbye.

For months we kept freedom riding until one day, I got a message from a mate saying, 'Police are waiting to arrest you when you get off the train.' We got off and there was a whole line of police and revenue collectors. They said, 'No one comes past unless you show us a valid ticket.' We refused.

The average age of our group was late seventies, so what did the police do? They charged us. I was arrested, we had a woman in a wheelchair that got knocked over and a guy in our group was pulled down with his legs splayed out, head pushed on the platform.

A few days before a mate and I were due to appear in court, the case against us was abandoned. So, what did we do? The Freedom Riders rode into Sheffield on our court date and had a huge rally outside the court instead.

The local MP said, 'You're wasting your time, nothing can be done.' But during our campaign it was announced pensioners could ride half price and disabled passengers could ride free again, so that was something.

The police may hit us with their truncheons. But that doesn't mean we won't stand up for what we believe in and fight for what is right.

514: I SHINE FOR HIM

I wasn't brought up a Christian. My mum and my auntie went to church, but I thought, 'Well, they're all really old, aren't they? I'm young. I don't need to worry about dying and God and all that.'

Then, when I was in sixth form, a good friend of mine said, in the October half term, 'Do you want to come and visit my sister with me in Cambridge?' We went along and there were all these young people talking about God as though they knew him.

These were intelligent people who had got their A levels, and they were at Cambridge, and they were going to change the world, and they also actually believed in God. So that week, I became a Christian.

I went to Oxford, I studied French and German and in my mind, I was always going to live abroad. But God said, 'You're going to Goldthorpe.' I said, 'No, I don't want that.' And everyone said, 'Don't go there. It's not nice.' But when God calls you, you have to go where He says.

In the Bible when people found out Jesus came from Nazareth, the comment was, 'Well, does anything good come out of Nazareth?' People always say, 'What good comes out of Goldthorpe?' Brian Blessed maybe. We're mostly known for that BBC documentary about fly-tipping, and the burning effigy of Margeret Thatcher that was paraded down Goldthorpe High Street when she died.

But through the church we run so many groups. Parents and toddlers. Coffee mornings. Family fun days. Outings. And everyone here is an artist, you know. They wouldn't call themselves that, but they are. People knit and crochet and make things with their hands. The people. The people are so fiercely kind.

Now I love working in the community and being part of the community. Now I can't imagine doing anything else.

God wants us to be salt and light. He says in Matthew, Chapter Five, Verse Fourteen, 'You are the light of the world.' And to be the light of the world, you've got to shine. So that's it, I shine for me, I shine for my community, I shine for Goldthorpe. But mostly, I shine for Him.

645: TO INFINITY AND BEYOND

At quarter to seven there was a knock and I just didn't want to answer it. I opened the front door and a policeman was there with his car in the middle of the road, blue lights flashing.

I knew this policeman. We're a little village. His children went to the same school as mine, we'd say good morning to each other. When he recognised me, his whole face changed.

I got in the car and we set off at eighty miles an hour to Sheffield Children's Hospital. All the way there, I knew it wasn't good news. He said there's been an incident, a fire, and your boys are very poorly.

The officer did a handbrake turn outside the hospital. I ran through the doors and the first thing I saw was my son Paul receiving CPR. They said, 'We're going to have to let him go now,' and I said, 'No you can't,' and I took him in my arms. He looked at me and smiled, then his eyes turned grey.

A call came over to a police officer that the boy's dad had died in Barnsley Hospital. I can't imagine how those medics felt fighting for somebody who had tried to murder his own children. He'd lured them into the attic, barricaded them in and set fourteen separate fires in the house we used to share.

My son Jack was still fighting. I went to see him and his gorgeous thick hair was sticking out of these bandages. I just talked to him and said, 'Hang on, I'm here now. Keep going, be strong.' It was eleven o'clock at night when I watched them perform CPR. As I held Jack, I promised him no other child should have to die like this.

Police found out that in the fire, Jack had managed to get out of a hatch. When he realised his brother wasn't there, he went back for him. Jack was pulling Paul out of the attic, when he fell through the hatch and into the flames.

At St John's Church, the whole community came to wish the boys a final farewell. Everyone was holding arms, hands, elbows, anything to form a circle of love around the church.

The house was literally burned to the ground, but the community came together to rebuild. It needs to be a family home for someone else.

If I go out, people tap me on the shoulder or squeeze my hand and let me know they're thinking about Jack and Paul.

Whenever I dropped the boys at school, I said, 'I love you.' They always replied, 'To infinity and beyond.' Jack and Paul may not be here, but because of my community, that circle of love has carried on.

700: CLASSIC NORTHERN RAIL

Classic Northern Rail. Never the same platform, never the same time, always delayed. You'd think by now I'd have learned to expect chaos. But like going back to my ex, I always think, 'This time it'll be different.'

This one morning, I've got a big work meeting in Sheffield. An early start, well early for me – a seven a.m. train. I can't be late. I'm bleary-eyed, pumping music in my headphones to wake myself up as I walk to Barnsley Interchange. The sun still hasn't risen.

I get there half an hour early to make sure I definitely don't miss the train. I sit down on platform one – the trains to Sheffield absolutely always go from platform one – and I watch the clock. Six fifty-four. Six fifty-five. Six fifty-six. A Northern Rail guy pops his head onto the platform, looks at me, and walks back in.

I see a train on the opposite platform and at first don't think anything of it. That'll be the service going to Leeds.

Then, I look up at the board on my platform, and that's when I realise – there's nothing on it. No trains scheduled to stop. I look back across the platform, at platform two, and the dread hits me – is that my train?

I ask the guy who popped his head out. He grunts and nods. 'Great, thanks for letting me know.' I run like I've never run before – up the stairs, across the bridge, down the stairs and just as I'm about to make it onto platform two – the train pulls away.

This Northern Rail woman just looks at me and sighs, sympathetically. The Northern Rail guy on the other side of the platform is now on his phone. There'd been no announcements, no help, just me standing on the wrong platform for half an hour, watching the clock.

I know at this point, that's that. I'm going to miss my meeting. I look up at the board and get ready to count down another half an hour. The sun begins to rise over the tracks.

I text my boss to explain. She replies with an eye-roll emoji and the infamous three words that say it all: 'Classic Northern Rail.'

999: WHAT'S YOUR EMERGENCY?

If you don't get verbally abused down the phone at work, you've not been to work. I've been called an idiot, stupid, worthless, I've been threatened to be killed. I just have to go outside for five, take a breather and go back in. Headset on, 'Nine-nine-nine, what's your emergency?'

Some days we'll have about forty people taking calls for the whole of Yorkshire. We get calls from Barnsley, Huddersfield, Sheffield, Wakefield, Hull, Doncaster. And people just phone up with silly things like 'I've stubbed my toe' or 'I've got toothache'.

We have frequent callers all the time. This one guy calls about ten, fifteen, twenty times a day like, 'I need my window opening' or 'I want a hot meal' or 'Can you get me a drink?' I have to laugh, I mean you can hear his carers in the background saying, 'Get off the phone, you don't need an ambulance.'

The amount of mental health calls we take is crazy. I've had calls from people who've overdosed, calls from people who've hung themselves while on the line. We can't send an ambulance straight away. The wait time is three hours. So, by the time we've got there, some people have already done it. I tell myself it's not real. Like, if I can't see it, then it's not real.

There are some calls that get you though. This one time, I had to leave my desk on a call with a gentleman who was stood on the top of a bridge. I was on the phone for an hour trying to talk him down. When he came down, he just broke down in tears hugging the police. The guy just wanted someone to listen. Someone to care.

After that, I went back to work. Go outside for five, take a breather, go back in. Headset on, 'Nine-nine-nine, what's your emergency?'

1,000: STILL BORN

Sarah was only given a certificate of death. She never got a birth certificate.

The path is covered with oak trees. I remember going up it, conker picking as a kid. I'd follow the path through the ruins of the Abbey and up the hill. Tucked away in the right-hand corner there's a row of graves and a memorial.

Mum was sixteen when my sister Sarah was stillborn. It would have been quite difficult for her to speak about it back then. Hospitals used to bury babies in mass graves, stillborns didn't have funerals. Nurses just wrapped them up and bundled them away. If the baby didn't breathe, they weren't thought to have lived.

It's hard to remember somebody you've never met, but Sarah played a massive part in our lives. Mum always took us to the memorial for stillborns to mark every Christmas, birthday, Mother's Day. I'd take a flower and put it down, to remember my sister and the other children that have passed.

The memorial now is covered in moss. It's sinking and what have you. There's weather damage and things. Everybody deserves to be remembered. In Barnsley, there's thousands of babies like my sister. They're lying in unmarked graves, unknown. In the craziness of life, we need space to grieve.

I talk to my kids about my sister. They call her Auntie Sarah. Now my mum's passed on, I see it as my inheritance to reinstall that memorial and maintain that physical marker. My sister won't be forgotten. Those babies were here, their lives mattered.

Sarah was only given a certificate of death. She never got a birth certificate. A stillborn is still born, if that makes sense?

1666: BIG CHICKEN, LITTLE CHICKEN

Park up, scan through doors, gates open, in you go. Look up at the big signs. 'Bigger. Better. Stronger. Fitness just got serious.'

Head straight to changing rooms. Full of men, spending lots of time standing naked in front of each other. Flexing muscles.

Go to locker, swing in the combination code, I'll give you a clue, it's the Great Fire of London. Then, that's it, hit the floor.

Floors full of men, spending a lot of time making big loud grunting noises. When I hear them, sometimes I think, 'Wow, if that's the noise you make when you lift, what noise do you make when you – you know?'

So I'm there, doing my arms, doing my dumb-bell presses, and there was this guy. I couldn't not notice him. Arms are like chicken drumsticks. Legs like little chicken legs. He was basically all chicken. Enormous, enormous guy. Like he'd walked out of Instagram. He was there with his mate, who looked like a much smaller, much skinnier chicken.

They were there squatting and lifting and pressing and grunting. And big chicken guy says to little chicken guy, 'Come on, come on, come on, keep going, keep going, keep going.' He's trying to push his friend, make him work for it, he won't let him stop.

He starts counting. 'Ten, nine –' counting, grunting, counting, grunting – 'eight, seven, six –' counting, grunting, counting, grunting – 'five, four, three, two, one'. Release. A huge final grunt.

And after the big finish I couldn't help glance up, look at them in the mirror. And I saw something I don't think anyone was supposed to see. Big chicken put his hand on little chicken. Right in the small of his back. It was very, very tender. Intimate. Loving. Then the grunting starts again.

1915: PUZZLES

I've always enjoyed doing jigsaw puzzles. Assembling pieces together to make a complete picture.

One rainy afternoon, my mum and I were tidying out a drawer when I came across a photograph of a handsome young soldier. He had thick black hair and the strongest-looking hands I'd ever seen in my life. I asked who it was and my mum replied, 'It's your grandad, George Bradley.'

Later that day, when our milkman called round for his money, I showed him the photograph. He said he'd known George as a workmate down the pit and remarked, 'We all called him Bull Bradley because he worked harder than anyone else.'

This was the start of my own unique puzzle.

I started by looking through old newspapers to find out more about George. I found this little news excerpt from when he was a lad. It was just before Bonfire Night. George and his mates had managed to procure some fireworks. He got in trouble with the police for letting them off in the street.

George was enlisted to the Barnsley Pals in 1915. But with his mining skills, he was transferred to the Royal Engineers, to do more specialist things. He'd be out using flamethrowers, which must have been pretty scary. He'd tunnel into no-man's-land and lay all these mines.

I knew the puzzle wasn't complete, so I kept pushing on.

Despite all his injuries, George survived the war. He married his sweetheart Ida, but all was not well. An uncle of mine said he'd see Grandad after work, standing outside the house with his head in his hands.

The local doctor referred George to a home for disabled veterans. His admission records said he was suffering from shell shock. He remained there until his death.

When I visit his grave, I think of that photograph and all that I've discovered since. I pray one day I'll meet George and the puzzle will be complete.

1957: PINK SUNSET

Maurice would sit behind the shop counter on a stool, wearing a powder-blue suit with a cigarette in a holder between his fingers. A swearing parrot could be heard in the back.

As a lad, I remember picking up a cabbage. Maurice stared at me from behind the counter and said, 'If you're not bloody buying it, put it back down.' You couldn't sit on the wall outside the shop and if you did, Maurice would run you off it.

When Maurice got het up about anything like that though, Fred would calm him down again. At first, we just thought they were business partners who lived together. I don't think we knew what homosexuality was back in 1957.

They met in the war, serving in North Africa. When Maurice set eyes on Fred it was love at first sight. He couldn't get Fred out of his mind. They fought together all through the war and saw many a sun set. When they were discharged, they wound up back in Darfield, right close to where Maurice was born.

Round here we don't care who you are, as long as you're decent. All the women wanted to dance with Maurice on a Saturday night. He wore a dinner suit, dickie bow, lipstick and make-up on his cheeks, a little bit of rouge.

Maurice was a cantankerous, grumpy, flamboyant, eccentric and opinionated man. Fred was gentler, but he could be tough as well. Their ashes are scattered in the churchyard, down the road from their shop.

Before he died, Maurice told us he wanted the shop to be turned into a museum of all his antiques. So that's what we did. It was derelict when we started, but over the years the people of Darfield have brought the place back to life.

There's a blue plaque that we're putting outside, to honour Maurice and Fred. On the plaque, we've engraved: 'To a loving couple, defying convention until their deaths. Let their pink sun never set.'

1980: THE WORRY

Me and my mate David, we were looking for something to do. It was the 1980s and there were two main areas in business. One wor computers and the other wor hospitality, and well, we knew nowt about computers, but because we drank a lot, went to the pub a lot, we thought we'd give hospitality a go.

You worry, you worry. Things might not work out.

We started looking but, well, turns out, pubs are very expensive. I'd heard about this guy who'd bought an old building and changed it into a pub. So I said, 'Well, if he can do it. Why not us?' I know now, that was, well, quite naive.

The worry, the worry, the worry.

When we first walked in it was all boarded up. High ceilings, big rooms, but a lot to do. And well, me and David looked at each other and we thought, 'Flippin' heck. We've spent every single penny we've got.'

The worry, the worry, the worry.

We started in September and we were still going in July. The day we started working on it, it started raining and the whole time, it didn't stop. We were there digging holes. It rained and rained and rained.

The worry, the worry, the worry.

That first night. That night we opened. We honestly didn't know what to expect. But, the world came. The whole world. I looked at David and David looked at me and, well, for just a moment, just a moment – the worry, the worry lifted. And we thought, 'Maybe, just maybe, we'll never worry again.'

1981: WHAT CONNECTS US?

I happened to be in town the day they lifted the railway bridge off. I watched as they took it clean away, like it had never existed.

What connects us? Who decides?

The Woodhead train line was as fast as anything. You'd get to Sheffield in a blink, and once you were in Sheffield you were in Manchester in no time at all.

What connects us? Who decides?

That track carried coal, carried workers, carried families between two sides of a hill that might as well have been a wall.

My grandad, he used to come through for work on that line. Travel from Hadfield to the other side of the hill. So did half the family at one time or another.

What connects us? Who decides?

I grew up in Derbyshire, but I knew I wanted to move for work. The Woodhead line meant I could cross the hill – Derbyshire to Yorkshire. I could move on and out, but still stay connected to where I came from. To my family – my old life.

What connects us? Who decides where gets a stop on a line? A decision that can dictate where you live, where you work, who you meet – sometimes even who you fall in love with.

I happened to be in town the day they lifted the railway bridge off in 1981. People don't realise what gets lost when a line closes. Not just transport. Connections.

1983: STAND YOUR GROUND

You know where them tower blocks in town are, just off Park Road? Well, a bloke told me they used to call it Bare Bones. Nobody there had owt. Nowt at all. Nowt. I lived there.

Stand your ground, fight, don't let them win.

My first fight was in school and there's nowt to tell. It was over in seconds. I go for the nose, it's like hitting the off button. It makes their eyes water and hurts like hell.

Stand your ground.

Left school for a poxy little job in a car manufacturing company. Hundreds applied. That's how bad it wor in 1983.

Fight.

My brother was an angry young man, he made me look like a saint. I walk in the foyer of this club and there's this kid with his face split, he wor just a mass of blood. I said to my girlfriend, 'My brother's done that.' I go upstairs and sure enough, there my brother wor.

Don't let them win.

Dad is drunk standing over me. That man wor a drinker, down the pub for seven days a week and he's erupting at me, 'I'm going to stove your face in, kick you round ginnel hole.' I lift my foot and kick him. He hits the door and falls. I get thrown out. I wor nineteen.

Stand your ground, fight, don't let them win.

I move in with my auntie, it's quiet. I watch Christmas adverts on telly. They say one thing but the reality is another. Who has a table full of food and a family that looks like that?

Dodge.

I don't regret scrapping, no, I'd do it all again. These days though I prefer to dodge. It hurts a lot less.

1990: RASPBERRY BERET

Being a woman in Barnsley, if you want to be creative, you have to fight.

Auntie Gwen had such bad asthma that she couldn't smell. I think that's why her sight was dialled up. It took over her senses.

Everything my auntie wore or made was popping with colour, colour, colour. She always wore a bright, raspberry beret.

She made my confirmation dress when I was thirteen. And that's how I knew my Auntie Gwen – as a dressmaker. She was *the* dressmaker for the whole village.

It's only getting older I learnt – we saw her as a dressmaker, but she saw herself as something different. Since she was fourteen she knew, she absolutely knew, an artist is what she wanted to be.

She loved fine art but she was told, 'Fine art is for men. Stick to embroidery. Stick to making dresses.'

Being a woman in Barnsley, if you want to be creative, you have to fight.

As a girl, I would go round to her house and it was full of art. A fabric collage she'd made with rows of bright Redfearn's chimneys. A linocut print of colourful cats, her favourite creature. A doll she'd crafted and made from scratch, that would tell me stories. Walls full of colour, colour, colour – letting visitors know, in her own house, in her own way, she hadn't given up fighting.

As I got older, the art came from inside her house to out. It was the 1990s. She went to Barnsley College. She studied fine

art and started making the art she'd always wanted to make.
She was in her seventies but she was determined

We buried auntie Gwen in her bright, raspberry beret.
A woman who, until the end, and no matter who was trying
to dull her, was always popping with colour, colour, colour.
A creative woman who knew – it's never too late to fight.

1995: THE BIG WHEEL

The wheel of life, it moves.

Growing up it wor obvious that my dad didn't like me.
I never knew why. He just took a dislike to me and that wor that. It meant I grew up left out, lonely, different. When I wor older I just knew I wanted to foster.

The wheel of life, it moves.

It was a long, long assessment. You have to go back to your earliest memory. They scrutinise and analyse every detail of your life. I got approved in May 1995. Since then, I've fostered fifteen young people.

The thing about trauma is, it can look like so many different things. It can mean screaming, thrashing, trashing the bedroom. Or it can mean going withdrawn, not wanting to talk.

The key is to never take it personally. No matter what, I make sure those young people never feel left out, never feel lonely, never feel different. I make sure they know they're wanted. They're liked.

The wheel of life, it moves.

Lauren moved in when she wor thirteen. She didn't speak for the first six months. She didn't want to be living with me, she wanted to be back with her family. Very, very slowly, very, very gently, we started to form a bond.

She'd hardly been to school at that point. Very, very slowly, very, very gently, I said, 'The world's your oyster, you know. You can achieve anything you want to achieve.'

Life's not easy. It's like a big wheel. Sometimes you're at top. Sometimes you're at bottom. But that wheel of life, it always moves.

My dad never helped me move that wheel, but in a way that's the best gift he could have given me. I move that wheel myself.

Last summer, I watched Lauren graduate from university. It wor the proudest moment of my life.

I tell every young person I foster, 'You can move that wheel, you know. The wheel of life, it always moves.'

2000: HAPPY NEW YEAR

Ten!

The grown-ups kept saying it was a once-in-a-lifetime opportunity. My grandma used to watch the news religiously and they kept on talking about this giant Dome they were building in London.

Nine!

I was seven and I was obsessed with our new computer. I had this game on a floppy disk – *Command and Conquer*.

Eight!

They started talking on the news about the Millennium Bug – that when the year turned from 1999 to 2000 the clocks might stop. Planes might drop out of the sky and worst of all, computers might crash. I thought, 'Oh no – I'm going to lose all the levels on my game.'

Seven!

My nan kept saying not to worry. That life had existed before computers, so it will learn to survive without them again. She said they'd not needed computers when we beat Hitler.

Six!

We had a special tea – fish and chips and gravy. You knew it was an important occasion when the chips were home-made. It was me, my two older brothers, my younger sister, my mum and my nan.

Five!

I couldn't believe how late I was allowed to stay up. We were all snuggled together watching the telly, watching the

Millenium Dome, watching London bring in the New Year like it was theirs. The new century was for them and we were getting to watch it from our sofa.

Four, three, two, one!

The clock struck midnight. And suddenly I remembered. I ran, the fastest I've probably ever run, upstairs to the computer. I held my breath, turned it on. And there was my game. All my levels still there. Nothing lost. Everything the same.

When I came downstairs my family had stopped watching telly. They were up, off the sofa, and looking out the window. You could see fireworks across all of the fields. Lighting up the night sky. Colours blasting into the air – red, blue, yellow, amber.

We weren't watching someone else anymore, we were right here, in Barnsley, and the New Year was ours. I'd never seen so much light in darkness.

Happy New Year.

2007: LET THE FLOOD IN

It was during the night of my sixtieth birthday when it happened. We had a little Yorkshire Terrier called Chloe at the time. She was an old dog who was totally blind but she knew something was wrong. When it started to rain, Chloe was just sat on a chair in the dining room, shaking. She'd never done that before.

I looked out my window and honestly, the heavens just opened. I put some towels down on the floor, just in case there was a leak. But then it slowly dawned on me, towels weren't going to cut it.

The garden started to fill up with water and I couldn't believe my eyes. Water was coming up through our wooden floors and it was filthy, like mud. I watched as the living-room carpet started to float.

The river that runs near our house had burst its banks and the gates in the garden were about to buckle. My husband looked at me and we realised, there was no point fighting it. We went to the gates and one by one, we opened them up and let the flood in.

We took Chloe upstairs and settled in for the night. Out the window, I saw boys climbing the fence to our house and I was screaming at them, 'Be careful, if you fall, you'll drown!' Four-by-fours and lorries were driving past – pushing water into our house. I was waving at the drivers to slow down, but they didn't take any notice.

The next morning, my husband, Chloe and me stood at the top of the stairs. We lost a lot that day. All our furniture, my husband's stamp collection and some of our memories. But we were all safe and that's the main thing. You can't replace people, but you can replace things. Do you know what I mean?

One thing I do remember is cooking a fillet steak. We were supposed to have it the day after my birthday, as a special treat. So, I put on my wellies, tried the grill and it worked! I was sliding round the kitchen, shouting up the stairs to my husband, 'Do you want cheese with it?'

I've never felt so powerless as the day the flood came. But sometimes all you can do is crack on, smile and see the funny side. Sometimes all you can do is let the flood in.

2013: IRON LADY, REST IN RUST

We had an assembly at school. We learned about the pits and the anguish of the strikes, and it was all, 'Now children, I know a lot of you are going to be out with your parents tomorrow evening so you need to be careful and stay away from fire.'

That weekend I went round to Grandad's for tea. We had something to eat and then he said, 'Get your shoes and your coat on. We're off up the road to witness some history.' Down Frederick Street, up the High Street and onto the end of the bridge. Flyers were stuck on over the lamp posts advertising the parade.

It was all anticipation, people whispering, and then I heard them coming. You know in the war films, there's like a battalion and there's a drummer at the front? At the back of the parade was a coffin and an effigy of Maggie Thatcher.

My grandparents took me to get a better view. Loads of people were walking up the road singing and cheering, 'Milk snatcher,' 'Iron Lady, rest in rust,' 'Ding dong, the witch is dead,' and all that stuff.

The parade went right up to this brownfield site directly next to the Goldthorpe pub which watered all the miners as they came out the pit. A place the community wanted to reclaim. Everyone had donated a piece of wood, so it all went on the pyre. A fire was lit and we all watched as Thatcher went up in flames.

That night my grandparents opened a very nice bottle of wine they'd bought during the strike. They'd always make sure my dad and my uncle had a good meal when they were kids. Grandma and Grandad would then have whatever was left. They'd sit in the cold and survive on what they could.

All these years they'd saved that bottle of wine. So with a full glass each, my grandparents made a toast to the pits and to the passing of the witch.

Growing up, I always felt this cloud of hurt weighing down on me. This cloud of grief and loss and betrayal. Thatcher's dead. What do we do now?

2015: REBUILD MY LIFE

I always tell everybody, 'It's never the end. It's always just the beginning of your next life.'

Rebuild my life when I leave home at the age of sixteen to join the army. Rebuild my life when I leave the army. The army left me paralysed. My wife says I'm not a man anymore. I wake up one morning and she has a knife in her hand. Stabs me in the groin. Says she doesn't believe I'm paralysed. I have to leave. I become homeless.

Rebuild my life when Help 4 Homeless Veterans get me a flat. I'm down South but the flat's in Barnsley. I'd heard all the stories, 'Oh it's grim up North. Nothing but ex-mining.' All of that. But they've got me a flat so off I go.

My first day, I get cigarettes out my pocket, I'm rolling along smoking. This guy comes up behind me, taps me on the shoulder. I think, 'Here we go.' He hands me a tenner and says, 'You dropped this.' I couldn't believe it. That would never happen down South.

I meet Diane. The beginning of my next life. I make her a promise that I'll make her laugh every single day. She was all about love. Putting love out.

I say to them, at Help 4 Homeless Veterans, 'Whenever someone new moves here, will you send them my way? I'll meet them. We'd have them round.' I mean like Christmas, we'd have twenty people round in our two-bedroom flat. Diane making them all food. Love. Put love out. Wherever you can.

Before Diane died she made me make two promises to her. That I would carry on living. And that I would find love again. So here I am, again, rebuilding.

I tell myself what I tell everybody else, 'Whatever you're going through, it's never the end. It's just the beginning of your next life.'

2017: CHEERING FOR ME

You never used to see a man doing any sort of exercise round Barnsley. In town, you'd get stabbed for wearing Lycra back then. But bit by bit, it started creeping in. On the roads in the town centre there'd be a little flash of neon here, a little hi-vis jacket there.

I had this absolutely knackered old bike. Squeaky brakes, saggy tyres, but I thought. 'Look, let's just give it a go. What's the worst that can happen?' At that time, I had more love handles than handlebars so I would go out first thing in the morning, and just hope and pray I didn't see anyone I knew.

It was 2017 and I'd sort of vaguely heard about them starting the Tour de Yorkshire. But I mostly remember thinking, 'No way. That will never catch on.' The hills are too big. The people are too fat. After that, I must have just forgotten all about the Tour de Yorkshire. I definitely didn't have the date in my diary, let's put it that way.

This one morning, I overslept. Missed my morning cycle. But I had a wave of courage. I thought, 'Look, just go out on your bike this afternoon. What are the chances of seeing anyone?'

I'd got to the top of a hill and hit a junction – like, a fork in the road. I turned right. I must not have looked behind me properly. Because I heard them before I saw them. They sounded like the wind.

This huge, enormous wave of cyclists came pouring past me. And proper cyclist too. Lycra. Helmets. Clip-on shoes. And there I was, in the middle of them all, in my grey tracksuit bottoms and pyjama top.

That's when I started hearing the cheering. I lifted my eyes up and ahead of me there were crowds. Big crowds. Cheering. Cheering us all on. I got this rush of adrenalin and I thought, 'Sod it. I'm going to enjoy this.'

I peddled as fast as I could. There was this one woman, she started running alongside my bike. She was cheering and whooping – for me! I lifted my hands in the air and cheered myself. I felt like king of the world.

As soon as we hit the next junction, I turned off. I was gasping for breath, drenched in sweat, but I'd done it. I didn't win, I didn't finish, I mean technically, I wasn't actually even in the race. But for thirty glorious seconds, someone thought I was. Someone was cheering for me.

2022: SAME HOUSE, SEPARATE LIVES

I was born in Freetown, Sierra Leone, where there is all life.
Late night music playing in the clubs and into my home. My
wife came here to study, she wanted me to come with her.
So I left my country and we move to Jump, Barnsley. When
I arrived, the intimacy ended.

I prayed to God, asking the Lord to help me.

Life was hell. I felt like I was in prison, like I might explode.
I was born and grew up with this principle – marriage is sacred,
a circle, a bond. Husband and wife must have one direction. If
I am with you, we must work towards one goal. Me and my
wife lived in the same house, but we lived two separate lives.

I prayed to God, asking the Lord to help me.

In the mornings, I made the breakfast but the only thing we
shared was a kitchen table. You live in your room. I live in
my room. We speak sometimes, sometimes no talk. I worked
on it, I do not quit. So many sleepless nights.

I prayed to God, asking the Lord to help me.

I have a hot temper, and I don't have friends. I'm always
afraid to hurt people and I don't like people hurting me. At
work I felt alive, but walking home, my soul felt dead.

I prayed to God, asking the Lord to help me.

I found the messages and recordings on her phone. I told her
plain, 'It's finished, it's done. You broke something sacred,
the circle, the bond.' I moved out without looking back.
I remember the year, it was 2022.

We were together for years and years. I prayed to God, and
the Lord answered. It just took time.

2025: MOON MAGIC

I love the moon. I mean, it controls tides and periods – what's not to love?

Each full moon, I do something small. I don't howl or anything, but I'll, you know, write down my hopes and dreams. Sometimes read them out loud. Sometimes, if I'm feeling fancy, light a candle. Each full moon feels like a new beginning.

I'd seen on the news there was gonna be a lunar eclipse. On the seventh of September 2025. With a solar eclipse it can only be seen by a small number of people in a small number of places. But with this lunar eclipse, you'd be able to see it from anywhere on the night side of the Earth. That meant people in Africa, Australia, Asia and Europe – people so far away from each other in all different parts of the world – we'd all be looking up at the same sky. Seeing the same thing. How magical is that?

The internet was saying to get up somewhere high. I remembered, I'd tried to do parkrun at Locke Park once. I'd had to stop because of the killer hill. Perfect.

I packed a picnic blanket, some sandwiches, a flask of tea and I told my boyfriend, 'Get in the car. We're going to see the lunar eclipse.' He's really not into this kind of thing. But, luckily, he's really into me.

We parked up and walked to the highest part of the park. At the top of the hill, you can only see out in one direction. In front of you, you can see for miles and miles. But behind you, it's all trees and buildings and blocked.

It wasn't long before we realised the moon – yeah, the moon was behind us.

I said, 'That's that, then. A sign of what a terrible month it's going to be.' I was ready to go home and eat the sandwiches in front of the telly. But my boyfriend, once he's started something, he finishes the job. He said, 'Get in the car. We're finding you that moon.'

He set off driving. And as we drove, the land it sort of – opened out. All around us, we could see everything. And the sky, the sky was pink.

I plugged my phone into the speakers and put on *Star Wars* 'Ride of the Valkyries'. We drove around like that for about half an hour. And I thought about everyone else, far away, looking up at the same night sky.

We didn't find the moon. But you know what, it didn't matter. I may not have seen the moon that night but I saw the silly things my boyfriend is willing to do to make me happy. And how magical is that?

2066: ORGREAVE

Working class people never get to write their own history, our history is written for us.

My parents were part of Militant Labour, a radical part of the Labour Party. I didn't really have much choice with my politics, I learned them on my mum and dad's knee.

For school, we'd have to write a sort of scrapbook about what we've been up to in the summer holidays. Most kids were like, 'Oh, we went in the caravan to Whitby,' or whatever. I'd been dragged off to an anti-nuclear demonstration or picket line somewhere.

I'm what people describe as one of Thatcher's children. In the hall outside my bedroom we had this big poster of her. Hands outstretched, she had blood running through her fingers and images of the miners. I remember getting up in the night to go to the toilet, terrified of it.

Mum's got boxes of campaign stuff. In one of these boxes is a picture of me and my brother at the Christmas Pantomime with Coal not Dole badges on our school jackets.

As I got older, I started attending Durham Miners' Gala, reading books about the strike and seeing the images for myself. I'll never unsee the pictures of the battle at Orgreave Coking Plant. Police dogs, riot gear, huge truncheons, horses charging. Miners that were arrested that day were refused medical treatment. Pools of vomit and blood, broken arms, broken skulls. A crime and a police cover-up.

A group of us came together, to campaign and fight for justice. We got T-shirts, leaflets, a bank account, a Facebook page and it just grew from there. The government has embargoed the documents of Orgreave until 2066, but we won't wait that long.

In Barnsley we still live with the scars of the strike. Many of us now work on the sites of former pits in call centres on minimum wage. If we don't dispel the myths and prove what's been done to us is unjust, the past will repeat itself.

Working-class people never get to write their own history, our history is written for us. It's time to rewrite the story ourselves.

4,000: POLSKA BIBLIOTEKA

I always have two books on the go. One in English, one in Polish. I just need to keep both languages going.

Dad never talked about the Gulag, the camp, apart from when we tried to throw food away. If you'd had one slice too many and tried to sneak it off your plate, Dad used to say, 'That's the difference between life and death. Give it to the dog, give it to the birds, but do not put it in the bin.'

When I was a kid, someone gave my dad a rabbit and my mum made a stew. Dad caught me turning my nose up at it, so he says, 'There's nothing wrong with that, it tastes like chicken. Now you don't want a fox stew, fox tastes lousy.' I remember thinking, 'When did my dad eat a fox?'

I grew up learning Polish, there was never any question about that. I was always being told that we were going to go back and help rebuild the country after the war. 'I did not fight for my country to live abroad' – that was my father's phrase.

Dad was considered an enemy of the state. He expected communism to burn out in a few years but it didn't. Over time, Dad talked less and less about going to live back home. Until he stopped talking about it at all.

For years I was one of the few people in Barnsley who could speak Polish. But then, the next generation arrived to work in our warehouses, our kitchens, our care homes. All of a sudden, my phone was ringing at all times of the day and night with people asking, 'Can you translate this form?' or, 'Can you help me fill this in?'

I opened up a library and a drop-in centre to help with translation and give these people somewhere to go. At Polska

Biblioteka we must have nearly well over four thousand books by now.

I asked one little boy who comes to us why he wanted to learn Polish. He said, 'When I speak to Grandma in English, she doesn't understand. I come here to learn Polish so she doesn't cry.' Speaking Polish helps us understand each other. I suppose it helps us understand ourselves.

As a family, we never went to live back in Poland, but I always have two books on the go. One in English, one in Polish. I just need to keep both languages going.

60,000: CLASSROOM WINDOW

I didn't think I'd get in. I just applied because my teachers told me to. Two or three of them kept pushing it, non-stop talking about this scholarship all the time. So, I thought, 'All right, I'll put in an application and give it a go.'

In my personal statement, I had to explain my life to them. I wrote about Scouts, Duke of Edinburgh, volunteering and all the random things I did. They also had some questions like 'What is your family like?' 'Why do you think you'd be a good fit for boarding?'

Eton is otherworldly. It's like a village with cottages, a few shops and this huge college in the middle. You can't get away from it. I was in a group of twelve boys who'd been shortlisted, and we were from literally everywhere in the country.

There's this big clock tower in this courtyard. Next to it is a building with a room full of computers. That's where we did the exams. One of the questions was, 'Imagine what would happen if everyone in the world knew everything?'

I kept refreshing my phone, waiting for the news. When it finally arrived, there was a long, long page and I was skim reading all the way down until I found out, I was awarded a place. Most boys pay for everything, it's like sixty thousand pounds a year, but this letter said they'd fund everything for me, apart from my shoes.

I've got the pinstripe trousers, the white shirt, waistcoat, big tailcoat and an overcoat for the winter. The only fiddly bit is the detachable collar. It's weird to put on unless you know how to do it. Some boys get bow ties, I can't imagine trying to get that on quickly in the morning.

It didn't hit me until the car was loaded and I was ready to go. I packed my posters and a picture of my girlfriend and me at prom. This September, I thought I was going to Barnsley College with my mates. I didn't think I'd be going to Eton. I used to see fields outside my classroom window. Now I see Windsor Castle.

1,000,000: THE BEAT OF MY HEART

Everyone told me how hard pregnancy is. I loved being pregnant.

She's inside of you, hearing your heartbeat going at a million miles an hour – it's a sound so deep inside of you, but for her it's hard to ignore.

Everyone told me how hard birth is. I loved giving birth.

I walked, walked, walked around between contractions. I told myself, 'You can do this, you can do this, you can do this.'

The pain – it's unexplainable pain. Unforgettable pain. But then at the same time, you immediately forget it. As soon as you see your baby, all that pain goes away and it's absolutely worth it.

She was so big and bright and beautiful, eating the nurse's towel.

Five days after giving birth, I moved to Barnsley. Everyone told me, 'Barnsley is awful.' But I love Barnsley.

In the Caribbean, you step outside your house everyone says, 'Hi, hello, good morning.' I did have to learn, that isn't so much the thing in England.

My daughter has taught me so much.

She has this personality. She's bold, she's confident, she's – I suppose she's everything that I would love to be. And I'm trying. Because I think, I think I have that personality too. It's just deep, deep inside of me.

Whenever we're around town, she runs up to someone, touches their scarf, touches their glasses, says hi. She will build a little bond between her and that other person and you know, then I can build that bond too.

I thought, you know, 'I'm going to say hi, hello, good morning to my neighbours', you know. Whenever I see them, even if they don't say it first. I started saying it and now, whenever they see me, they always say it back. Now, whenever they see me out and about they say, 'Hiya love.'

When my daughter sleeps she always wants to be near me, and she always sleeps best on my left side. I've realised it's because she wants to be near the sound of my heartbeat, going a million miles an hour. That's what she heard when she was inside of me, that's what she knows, what comforts her. She loves the beat of my heart.

Afterword

MADE IN BARNSLEY

Barnsley – or 'Baaaaaaarnsley', as non-locals tend to call it – is a town often misunderstood. The dominant narrative of Barnsley, presented by those who've never been here, sounds very different to the stories told by those who call 'Tarn' home. Sadly, our voices are rarely heard beyond the borough.

That doesn't mean to say we Barnsley folk sugarcoat our town – quite the opposite, as the vignettes in this book show. But between the gritty and the grim – the violence and the scars; the borders and the boarded-ups – there's those lesser-spotted shards of light and laughter, too. A Christmas countdown in Thurnscoe. Dancing in Monk Bretton. A flying kebab in Barnsley Town Centre.

During her 'Arts for Everyone' lecture at the Royal Shakespeare Company on 20 February 2025, Culture Secretary Lisa Nandy said: 'While talent is everywhere, opportunity is not.' It reminded me of a story I read a couple of years ago, when an audience member at York Theatre Royal's staging of *As You Like It* walked out mid-performance and asked for a refund. The cause? Actors speaking in Yorkshire accents.

An (ironic) aside: today's Yorkshire dialect has a closer resemblance to Shakespeare's own speech than the King's English we tend to hear on stage and screen. How fortunate us 'Tarn' folk are, against this backdrop, to have an opportunity to present our stories – in our own voices – between the covers of this book.

Just as importantly, these stories have been co-produced by a brilliant group of students from Barnsley College who also have a strong connection to Barnsley, and a desire to present the town in its own image. I was fortunate enough to return to Barnsley College – the same place I did my own A-Levels back in 2012 – and meet the young Creative Associates who made this *Calling Barnsley* project possible.

In my experience, creating an authentic story is as much about the person asking the questions as it is about the person answering them. These stories, then, are truly made in Barnsley. May they be heard not only in Thurnscoe and Monk Bretton, but also far beyond.

Dr Ryan Bramley
University of Sheffield, 2025

Get Support

If you, or someone you know, has been affected by some of the themes in this book, the following organisations may be able to help:

Childline

Childline is here to help anyone under nineteen in the UK with any issue they're going through. You can talk about anything. Whether it's something big or small, our trained counsellors are here to support you. Childline is free, confidential and available any time, day or night. You can talk to us.

Call 0800 1111

Visit www.childline.org.uk

Samaritans

Samaritans works to make sure there's always someone there for anyone who needs someone. Whatever you're going through, call us for free anytime.

Call 116 123

Email jo@samaritans.org

Visit www.samaritans.org

Resources

If you'd like to find out more beyond *Calling Barnsley*, we recommend the following resources:

LUNG

To download education packs for schools, watch recordings of a selection of our productions or listen to our podcasts, visit www.lungtheatre.co.uk/resources

Women's Aid

If you are the victim of domestic abuse, you can access a survivor's handbook and a forum to speak to other women by visiting www.womensaid.org.uk. You can also read *For My Boys* by Claire Throssell, published by Mirror Books.

HOPE not hate

For practical advice on how to build stronger communities, visit www.hopenothate.org.uk